THE LEGACY
OF SUN YATSEN

A HISTORY OF THE CHINESE REVOLUTION

BY GUSTAV AMANN

With prefaces by

KARL HAUSHOFER, PH.D., MUNICH

and

ENGELBERT KREBS, D.D., FREIBURG

Translated from the German by

FREDERICK PHILIP GROVE

NEW YORK & MONTREAL

LOUIS CARRIER & CO

TYPOGRAPHY BY R. S. JOSEPHY
JACKET DESIGN AND DECORATIVE END-LEAVES BY JOHN M. MEEKISON
PRINTED AT RAHWAY, N. J., IN THE UNITED STATES
BY QUINN & BODEN CO., INC.

SHEN-SI

SHAN SI

SHAN-TUNG

HO-NAN

KIANG-SU

NGAN-HWEI

NANKING

SHANGHAI

HU-PE

HANKAU

HAN-YANG • WU-CHANG

NINGPO

YO-CHEU

CHE-KIANG

TAI-CHEU

HU-NAN

NAN CHANG

WON-CHEU

KIANG-SI

FU-CHEU

FU-KIANG

FORMOSA
·JAPAN·

KWANG-SI

CANTON

HWEI-CHEU

AMOY

-TUNG

SWATOW

WHANG POA

KAULUN

HONG KONG

KWANG-

MACAO

SOUTHERN CHINA

Edward Pfau
351 West 34
New York City
New York
10 February 1947
Columbia University
T.C.
R.H. Macy
Co. Herald
Square

THE LEGACY
OF SUN YATSEN

CONTENTS

ILLUSTRATIONS

*The jacket design is from a lithographed
reproduction of the death-mask of
Sun Yatsen*

TRANSLATOR'S NOTE

WITHOUT identifying himself with any views propounded in the present volume—partly because he disagrees, partly because he simply does not know—the translator advised publication of this work of a German because he found in it a picture of a great subversion in modern history which, to say the least, is striking and novel. It seemed to him that the book, quite apart from its historical value, presents a struggle for freedom which is symbolic of the Promethean nature of man. No desire for propaganda was among the motives which prompted his labour.

F. P. G.

PREFACE OF THE AUTHOR

WHOEVER writes a book on present-day things must, in the composition, be led by his own judgment on the events or by the judgment which led the actors. Within the period of the Chinese revolution here pictured, initiative rested at first with Sun Yatsen, later with his immediate associates and friends. I have myself seen how the convictions of these people determined the events; and therefore I have made the content of this book quite dependent on the judgments and views of the actors in the Chinese drama. Had I allowed myself to be led by my own opinion, the book would sound different in many passages. But, as compared with the fact that, by a rendering of the motives of the leading personalities, I could, from the most intimate knowledge, give the reader a key to a real understanding of the revolution, it

xi

seemed to me inessential what my own opinions might be.

In order to confuse such an understanding as little as possible, I have suppressed Chinese names of all such personalities as enter only occasionally upon the stage. The names of the leading actors I have given, as do the Chinese themselves, by romanising Chinese letters according to English pronunciation.

Many a passage of the book I could have wished to treat more diffusely; much, to give with greater love. The limits of a volume forbade such procedure.

If I refrained from giving my own opinions, I wished all the more that every reader should form an impartial judgment on the happenings in the Far East.

GUSTAV AMANN

SUN YATSEN

Revolutionary and reformer of China

INTRODUCTION

THE advance of the Young-Chinese movement, from the establishment of the Kuo-Mintang government at Canton, to its almost magically swift spread to Shanghai-Wu-Chang and beyond the Yang-Tze-Kiang to the north, with the power of a fire prepared everywhere by scattered tinders, or of a dust explosion, and to the sudden break-down before Peking was reached—the event of 1925 to 1927—all that has today become history.

To have seen the event as an eye-witness and an actor; to have described it in all its inner motives, in a presentation which really penetrates the feeling of the Far East, that is the achievement of the author of this unique contribution to the history of what is perhaps the most remarkable part of the Chinese movement of renovation as far as it has gone. Only when seen in this light is it possible to put Amann's work in the

1

THE LEGACY OF SUN YATSEN

right place in contemporary history and to assign it
its due weight and value.

Nobody but a man who is at least nationally a
neutral—although he stood fully within the events—
could describe them impartially, could penetrate, as
an eye-witness, the innermost play of forces and yet
try, in describing things, to submerge his own personality in the purpose of elaborating the states of
mind and the motives of the leading men of an alien
race. To a Chinese, to anyone who belonged to the
race which fought in bitter civil war for the inner and
outer assertion of that race, such a relatively objective
description would have been impossible—no matter
whether he belonged to the group of heirs within the
family circle of Sun Yatsen, or whether he stood
near to Eugene Chen or to the left wing of wor-
shippers of the Russians or to Chiang Kaishek—the
only one with regard to whom the sense of justice of
the author seems to fail—or whether he belonged to
the Confucian and northern-Chinese circles following the spirit of the state-ideas of Yuan Shikai.
Predilection and inclination or aversion and hatred
would, consciously or unconsciously, have prevailed
where the narrator was so intimately connected with
the decisive struggle.

2

But even the Russian advisers, first so highly esteemed, then driven out, with Borodin and Galen at their head, were incapable of such commentaries of their actions. They have shown too clearly that they were partisan in the highest degree and would only fight from party battlements. Their international communistic doctrine and the hints received from Moscow were to them more than the success of the inner and outer liberation, than the cause of a nation of four hundred and fifty millions whose confidence had called them into a field of action to which only the highest freedom of the soul and utmost unselfishness could do justice. Still less, of course, was a report from the lofty height of history to be expected from the opponents engaged in the game of colonial imperialism.

This breach was filled by Amann who had once stood near Sun Yatsen as his friend; who had then shared with the heirs of Sun Yatsen, first their struggles, the days of their success and happiness, and then the days of doubt and downfall—faithfully standing by them, advising, acting, helping, co-operating without looking for advantage or fearing injury. And when the most significant part of the movement of Young-Chinese history since 1911 was dammed and on the point of hardening though still just fluid—when the group of his friends scattered—to Canton, to Moscow, into the camp of Chiang Kaishek, or into angry solitude—then Amann resolved to fix at least the closing picture of this onset. With a rich material of facts and pictures, he wants to state the inner motives and the forces at work in the outward happenings, speaking from his exact knowledge of the men and the events, before the facts—as Jan Hamilton said of the truth of immediate impressions gained on the battlefields of the Manchurian war—have slipped on their official cloaks.

In that, above all, lies the value of Amann's work. Where have we so far had such an unvarnished narrative of political and economic events in the Far East, based on a penetrating personal knowledge of all the acting personalities; seen, it is true, with European eyes, and yet founded on the Confucian maxim that all knowledge arises from love only? Whatever, during that period, was seen and described by eminent representatives of the nations powerful through their colonies, above all of the Anglo-Saxons (even by such prominent observers as Gilbert, Malone, Ransome, Rea, Sokolski) has never freed itself from the purpose for which it was written; in spite of honest endeavour it has never reached the relative independence of Amann. Amann is perhaps the first European who stood near enough to the events of 1926 and 1927 to understand them and to be able to describe them in their inner connections and who, at the same time, strove so honestly after justice and truth as to be able at least to adumbrate that truth through that whole web of legend and lie which hid it from contemporary eyes. It is true that he did not always succeed in grasping it firmly. To the opponent of the idealists in the Kuo-Mintang group, historically necessary though he be, above all to Chiang Kaishek, Amann cannot be just; nor to the Old-Chinese and the successors of Yuan Shikai. *That* the reader should know in advance. Therefore Amann's work needs to be fitted, with a few touches, into the totality of contemporary history in which, at the right point, it forms a necessary and indispensable link.

But for the prognosis of the Young-Chinese renovation it means much more; and in that consists the unique and personal feature of this contribution to the contemporary history of world politics. The description of the consequences of revolutionary events and of the mental and spiritual impulses released by them in exactly known personalities of the

5

Canton, Wu-Chang, and Nanking governments is a prognostic sign of the degree to which a great political idea is able to take hold of the Chinese masses and to which it can take effect in space.

This possibility has—in spite of the later downfall, brought about by inner disagreements between the leading political circle and the executive wielder of the power—proved to be far greater than all those who are said to know China would at first have admitted. Only through the lightning-quick occupation of the arteries of Shan-Tung by the Japanese; through the confusing attitude of Feng Yuhsiang and Yen Shishan of Shan-Si; and through the untimely inner quarrels about doctrine within the Kuo-Mintang, did the advance of the south against Peking fail; considered in the light of world politics, it failed, therefore, through chance things which, on another occasion, may not happen: and in spite of the opposite opinion of Amann and his friends, that advance was a prerequisite for a reorganisation of the whole Old-Chinese culture (perhaps without Manchuria) through the idea of the Kuo-Mintang.

The carrying power of the idea was, then, stronger than even its representatives believed to be the case. That they could not see what the soldier instinct of

Chiang Kaishek felt to be necessary—for that blind-
ness they had to atone heavily by the break-down of
their onset, magnificent as it had been. That the Russian advisers were not guided by the interests of
China but by that of their communistic doctrine, has,
it is true, not become clear to them even today.

But Amann's ability to feel his way so perfectly
into the state of mind, thus limited, of the Kuo-
Mintang leaders and to describe their situation in
such a way that this situation becomes clear, not only
to the retrospective historian of a generation hence,
but even to the politician who, by his action, advances
into the unknown, into circumstances still fluid, that
is his own, most personal achievement. Thus we can
investigate with unusual clarity—as we investigate at
an uncovered switch-board the wrong connections
made and the short-circuits as well as the possibilities
of avoiding them in future—the position of the wires
and the intentions of the wire-pullers within the
Young-Chinese magnetic field. Nobody else has so
far given us that possibility; and for that reason we
cannot pass this book by as a source of contemporary
history—even though it may waken all sorts of ob-
jections through the philosophy of life expounded
and defended in it regardless of consequences.

But what meets us here in an often uncanny way—
consciously opposing an idea which orients all things
by a European-American view—is not only the
author, but the state of mind as such of the leaders
of the south within the renovated China to which
Amann yields himself willingly in order to make their
motives clear to us. In very few great movements of
modern history have we so clear a discussion of what
was urging their leaders on, written almost at the
same time at which they took place. Amann's story
takes us from the struggle of the Chinese state social-
ism at Canton against the world-trade centre of Hong
Kong, to the advance, through Hu-Nan, against Hu-
Pe, through Kiang-Si against Fu-Kien and the
mouth of the Yang-Tze, including Shanghai; via the
political and military organisation of the trade unions
and of the peasant movement, to the temporary transfer of the government to Wu-Chang and to the
miracle of the organisation of three hundred millions
within the frame of the south; to the partial capitula-
tion of the great colonial powers before the renewed
spirit of China; and to the inner causes of its great
break-down following such a dazzling initial success.
It shows up the inner levers bringing about the
events, down to the intellectual and spiritual impulses

within the acting personalities; it does so, it is true, with predilection, but also without that false fear of "touching on prestige."

Only its immediate opponents were thrown under the dark shadow of the spot-light of the idea and thus perhaps appear blacker than is equitable; but fortunately we know these opponents from other sources quite accurately in their light and shadow: through Anglo-Saxon and Japanese observers; and through the caricatures of Russian literature on eastern Asia. What, without Amann, would be known to us only in misrepresentations, is precisely the nature of the actors in the astounding initial success of Young-China, in 1926 to 1927, as also of those who are to blame for the break-down, which was no less sudden, in the second half of 1927; it is the inner power of the strongest and purest impulse which, since 1911, has swept over and penetrated the huge Chinese country and the body of its people. What thus, led by such weak executive forces, but backed by the full strength of an idea understood by the people, came very near to being crowned by a liberating success, that will be possible again at any time: looked forward to with fear by the oppressors, with hope by those who are bound together by a common destiny, it has been

9

proved once for all as a possibility in world politics.

In the psychologic exposition of this possibility; in the insight into the soul of China—not as it was a generation ago, but as it is today and as it will be tomorrow—into the limits of its ability to make use of foreign helpers—as for instance of the dangerous Russian advisers—or to be thrown off balance by them: in that lies the great value of the unselfish narration of Amann in which his ego never obtrudes.

That is why I wished to help in making it prevail and to gain for it a hearing in the widest circles—in spite of the fact that my own political opinions often differ widely; for I consider it as one of the most important means to win an understanding for the Chinese movement of renovation, for the struggle of liberation within this great and old nation. The perplexities and throes of central Europe are much more closely akin to those of the Chinese than anyone thinks today. To understand the incarnations of great ideas which further mankind on its way, an incarnation brought about by strong idealism, within the power of mighty movements of nations and masses— even though they may not, in their first onset, lead to so considerable successes as, after all, fell to the lot of the Kuo-Mintang movement—to understand them and to work for them in their inner connections, that is the task of the hour in central Europe, too.

In this work of liberation, of a self-determination of national character, Amann is one of the most honest and faithful helpers even where we cannot agree with him in the choice of means; yes, even where lack of success has broken the staff over these means; with that in mind he gave his testimony to the most powerful movement of liberation which the present day has seen; a testimony which nobody can overlook or pass by who wants to see clearly in the political game of forces going on today in the farthest east.

KARL HAUSHOFER.

A WORD OF CRITICISM

I HAVE been asked by the author of this first European history, written "from the inside," of the Chinese revolution to jot down a few critical thoughts at which I have sometimes hinted in conversation with him while he was at work on the book. From the whole story it is clear that Sun Yatsen wanted to combine organically the Old and the New. His new spirit was a social and national spirit; in his Chinese nationalism he wanted to see what was best in the national spirit of China, Confucian morals, its family spirit, and the high value placed on spiritual things, as opposed to material things, saved and preserved for the new thing which was growing. Anti-religious, Russian-communistic ways, a bolshevist dissolution of the family and the hearth, were alien and hostile to his spirit. Yet he admired in Lenin the man who, as the author says, "had much suffered for his people; who had fought

13

for the poor man in the street and had conquered his heart for evermore." In the Russian revolution he saw the defeat of middle-class selfishness by the class-conscious bodies of workmen and peasants and the dawn of a new time. Sun Yatsen was a Christian; even in his last days he confessed himself to be a Christian. But never had he seen the organic power which binds heart to heart in the Christian *church*. Yes, the Christian powers showed themselves to him in China chiefly in unchristian egoism. It is tragic how, according to the story told by the author, he kept begging in vain for help to come, in his work, from Christian, that is, European powers. Nobody would understand him. Thus he allied himself with Lenin, he, the Chinese Christian, with the Russian pagan. It was an alliance of the greatest spiritual contradictions. While this alliance lasted, no organic growth could be fostered. In that I see the tragic guilt of Sun Yatsen committed against his own work.

The author describes with warmth how unselfishly and devotedly Borodin helped the southern Chinese, organising, building up, helping strategically. Neglecting all strictly bolshevist propaganda, Russian propagandist technique worked, according to him, for Sun Yatsen. The author, therefore, sees in the breach

with Borodin and the Russians, in the separation of
Chiang Kaishek from the Russians, a misfortune for
China: the "work of the militarists." The danger cannot be denied which lay in the break of 1927 between
southern Chinese and Russians: that experience
gathered by the Russians in China is going to make
their henceforth purely bolshevist propaganda among
the desperate peasants more effective than it could
have been without that experience of several years.
And since this propaganda will be addressed to
desperate and uneducated people, it will be the more
readily able to bring them under a dictatorship directed by Moscow. But I see the chief cause of this
danger not so much in the breach with the Russians,
brought about by Chiang Kaishek, as in the fact that
Sun Yatsen called upon the Russians to come to
China as organisers and propagandists. With them he
summoned a destructive power into his country which
was already sufficiently disintegrated. What is hap-
pening now is a consequence of *his* mistake. Just as
the government of the old German Empire was punished for the fact that Lenin and Trotzki were, in
armoured cars, sent through Germany to Moscow;
just as that same Empire was punished for allowing
Joffe to establish, as ambassador, a hearth of revolu-

tionary propaganda in imperial Berlin, thus Sun Yatsen's work was punished for the fact that he sought
an alliance with Lenin and allowed Borodin a large
sphere of action in China.

Germany conquered that bolshevist revolution
which began in 1918, with its soviets of workmen and
soldiers, as early as 1919, building from its ruins a
democratic republic by connecting it organically with
ancient culture. If Chiang Kaishek and his collaborators draw a lesson from that, they will be able to build
anew with the ruins. But they must be serious about
the *organic* connection between the new things and
the old.

That Sun Yatsen's Russian friends were not as
careful in their propaganda as the author believes,
becomes clear from his own statement that Chiang
Kaishek, as early as 1926, forced the "great number of
Russian communists within the administrative offices
of the nationalist government" to return to Russia, on
account of their "propagandist work for Russian communism"; and that even in 1927 one third of the central executive council of the national government was
of communist convictions. That, in connection with
the anti-religious revolutionising of the youth of
South China, permits us to draw the conclusion that

these friends called in by Sun Yatsen had after all begun to exert that *cultural* influence which he, in spite of all the similarities in organisation and national and social structure, would never concede to them. If "the work of the militarists" has deepened the thinning mark of division between Sun Yatsen's movement and Russian bolshevism till it marked a *hostile* division, then I, for one, see in that a gain for Sun Yatsen's bequest. It goes without saying that, in connection with that, there should be a cautious attempt at reconstruction in organisation and cultural endeavour—a reconstruction which denies itself campaigns of conquest and which allows that which has already been won to consolidate before it stakes everything on new, purely militaristic enterprises.

According to the narration of the author, Sun Yatsen provided for the growth of his new spirituality three periods: the militaristic period which is to ward off opposing enemies in order to make room within the country for the new movement; then the educative period which is to create order within the territory so far won and to educate the people up to the new ideas and their realisation; and the constitutional period as the final step. The present-day representatives of the government in South China must ap-

17

proach the task of the second period with that reverence for the organic life of a nation and for its spirituality which, in the field of religion, Catholic missions
show. Even the Jesuit missions of former centuries
methodically chose this way of connecting up rever-
ently with what had grown organically. If, in the details, they conceded too much; and if the missions,
therefore, perished in a war of rituals which broke
out as a consequence, yet the work of the missions as
resumed today has preserved the valid maxims which
are contained in that procedure of the ancients. To
my surprise I found at Tsi-Ka-Wei, in the library of
the Jesuits, the great collection of Chinese classical
literature which the learned fathers have established
there. It is said to be one of the most complete libraries
of Chinese classics in the world. With joy I saw at
Yen-Cheu-Fu in southern Shan-Tung the careful
work of the Steyl missionaries in the field of Chinese
lore to which they have devoted a number of valuable publications of their many-tongued press. But
the most perfect model for the procedure of the
southern Chinese in the second phase of their work
for Sun Yatsen's bequest I found in the Catholic
university of Peking which has been founded by the
Pope. That university is small. It is not yet of any
importance through its achievements. It is still in its

beginnings. But the idea from which it sprang should be a model for the executors of Sun Yatsen's will.

The university builds upon a three years' study of Chinese poets and Confucian moral philosophy. Literati of the old school give instruction. Thus the student is first familiarised with the spirit of his ancient culture without seeing in it anything final and perfect. Thence he is introduced into the world of new thought. A course in philosophy teaches him criticism with regard to what he has learned; it shows him the advantages and the weaknesses of Confucian morals: the possibilities of a natural motivation of goodness inherent in it, so that it can stand out against the destructive criticism of modern materialist thought; and the necessity of a completion and correction where the classics fail, above all in the estimation of women and of the ethnical unit as opposed to the over-estimation of man alone and of the family alone. Thus there arises the further task of a scientific foundation for a doctrine of society and state which preserves the inherited good and eliminates what is unwholesome. Finally, a philosophy of law and a jurisprudence built on natural law complete the structure of the temporal sciences.

But no culture can remain healthy without religion and theology. At a time when the ability to read and

the leaven of all sorts of religious and areligious movements in the life of the people rouses us from the naïve simplicity of times gone by, only a religion which has come of age and is guarded by a scientific theology can exist. That is the reason why the university of Peking is to have a theological department as soon as prerequisites are fulfilled and the forces are available.

This *organic* education, such as the Pope tries to make possible through the establishment of the Catholic university at Peking, seems to me to be the very thing which must be striven for in the south. By economic measures alone; by the organisation of a political and social party alone; by force of arms alone, such a task cannot be fulfilled: the task of giving a new form of life to a nation of four hundred millions who have suddenly been hurled into entirely new surroundings. "Except the Lord build the house, they labour in vain that build it." If for the second phase of the execution of Sun Yatsen's will, not *Moscow* but *the organically building spirit of Rome* is sought as ally, then there will be hope that China may be saved from that bloodshed and misery into which this unhappy country and nation seem plunged, at the time, beyond hope.

ENGELBERT KREBS.

20

SUN YATSEN AND HIS WIFE

THE LEGACY OF SUN YATSEN

THE daily press is almost the only source from which the public gathers information about events in China. The spasmodic turmoil and the difficulty of arriving at a survey of the happenings are responsible for the temptation to concentrate attention on mere externals. Curiosity, eager for sensation, prefers to devote itself to symptoms rather than to the causes of the mighty convulsions of the East. In the work of reporting, that seriousness which is due to the tragedy inherent in any revolution is, I am sorry to say, often wanting. At best the turn of events is represented as political or economic. Who, today, has an inkling that here is a great, ancient culture, hit in the innermost substance of its life by the hard drills of a western-European civilisation, which, in spite of subverting innovations fights on in a desperate struggle to pre-

23

serve that mode of life which was allotted to it by nature and hallowed by tradition?

The Germans like to call themselves a matter-of-fact nation. At a time when this word had not yet become so fashionable though it held perhaps more truth than it does today, the great economist Wilhelm Roscher wrote in his "National Economy," published 1854:

"The life of a people, like any life, is an indivisible whole, the manifold manifestations of which are connected by an inner bond. Whoever, therefore, wants to understand one side of it must know all sides; and, above all, there are seven sides which must be considered in this connection: language, religion, science, art, law, politics, and economics."

Wilhelm Roscher goes on to say:

"That even for the material interests the spirit of the people is the main thing, is proved by the example of the Chinese who have known printing, gunpowder, and compass for such a long time without, for all that, having acquired a clearly defined public opinion, a good army, and a respectable carrying trade."

Wilhelm Roscher has laid his finger on the very heart of things as they are in China; but that fundamental sentence of his, concerning the way to understand a nation, has found no acceptance. The question, Where does the consideration of the spirit of the Chinese people come in? is answered, even by Germans, and often with a smile of pity, "But let us be realists."

What should the spirit have to do with realities!

True insight should not permit us to call China simply a backward country. The fact that all western nations have endeavoured for decades, by their public opinion, by their considerable carrying trade, by their good armies, to bring to the Chinese that progress which the Chinese are often stubborn enough not to accept as progress, should hardly be a sufficient foundation for our pride.

It is true that even today China has no considerable carrying trade, no good army; but it has at last a public opinion.

What we understand of it is only the elemental way in which it finds utterance, not its contents. Perhaps this modest attempt to honour the theorem of Wilhelm Roscher will find enough readers who are interested in the reality of the public opinion of China.

The state of mind of the Chinese people at the time when Wilhelm Roscher printed his warning; the changes which have taken place since then in the spirit of the Chinese people; their consolidation into the present-day public opinion of China which is struggling for the recognition of the world; and finally, the consequences of this gigantic struggle, that is the subject of this meditation.

To begin with the end: the consequence of the loud and unanimous utterance of public opinion is an unyielding, decided, and energetic denial of all privileges to foreigners in China. The consequence of that denial is that the colonial supremacy of England is threatened—not to say at once that all foreign rule in Asia is threatened.

Intercourse between China and Europe is not, as might be supposed, a thing of today or of yesterday; our knowledge of the country is old. Pliny and Ptolemy mention that the ancient Romans imported silk, fur, and iron of peculiar excellence from China, getting them via the overland route, through Bactria and Persia; and in the annals of Canton (the Cattigara of Ptolemy) it is written, A.D. 168, "India, Arabia, and Rome brought *tribute* over the southern sea; and henceforward a lively trade sprang up with the foreigners."

Nor should it be believed that the relation of the Europeans to the Chinese has always been strained.

About 505 A.D. the Nestorians reached Canton by a sea route which had even then been used for a long time. At Hsin-Gan, in the province of Shen-Si, stands a stone into which they have carved their glorification of God and which bears testimony to the great favour which they had found with the emperors of the Tang dynasty. Marco Polo who visited the court of Kublai Khan at Peking about 1270 and who filled a high position in the state for years confirms the esteem and the friendship in which the Nestorians were held throughout the empire. Besides, Arabian travellers have left us word of the settlement of one hundred and twenty thousand Mahomedans, Jews, and Christians in China. Without let or hindrance these foreigners could travel and trade throughout the empire. Not before the beginning of the Manchu dynasty was the trade of foreigners restricted. But even under the Manchu emperors did the learned Jesuit fathers still enjoy high honour at the imperial court. When, however, the Dominicans and the Franciscans arrived and a violent quarrel arose between them concerning the Chinese name of God, the emperor K'ang Hsi forbade the Christian mission in China and sent the fathers home. The cause of the unpopularity of the European traders defined itself with the arrival of the Portuguese adventurers who, in 1516, came to Ningpo and Canton in their search for wealth. Their conduct was shameless. In 1573, for instance, they occupied without preamble the peninsula of Macao; and the Chinese were compelled to erect a barrier across the neck of the peninsula in order to keep these robbers at a distance. Soon after, Dutch vessels also appeared along the coast of China; but, repulsed by the Portuguese at Macao, they occupied the Pescadore Islands. Thence, dislodged by the Chinese, they landed at Formosa. They proved to be a troublesome pest for the Chinese along the coast of the province of Fu-Kien as well as for the Spaniards who had occupied the Island of Luzon (in the Philippines) in 1543, in order to trade along the Chinese coast. But not only they, the Spaniards as well showed themselves to be without shame in seizure and without respect for the Chinese.

The first English ship made its appearance before Canton in 1635. The Portuguese who were settled at Canton did their best to ruin the new-comers in the estimation of the Chinese. They wanted to be alone in sitting snugly next to their prey. The Englishman, it is true, lived up to the report given of him. He bombarded the Chinese forts at the entrance to the river and then withdrew. The East-India Company which, in England, had a monopoly for the trade in East Asia, traded up to 1678 with the cities of Amoy and Fu-Cheu on the coast of Fu-Kien. But to the Chinese, none of these guests were welcome any longer. They tried, by the imposition of a tariff and of high excise duties of various sorts, to spoil things for them; and at last, about 1755, the Chinese emperor issued a decree whereby only Canton remained to the foreigners as a trading port.

There, at Canton, alongside of the Portuguese, the English, Americans, and French now built their warehouses. The Chinese warded the foreigners off as best they could. Only specified Chinese business men, members of the Cohongs, received permission to trade with them; only through them could the foreigners have intercourse with the Chinese governor of Canton. To the governor, they were "barbarians resembling wild beasts who could not be ruled by the same principles as order-loving citizens."

Attempts on the part of Europeans to introduce more friendly relations into the trade were, on the other hand, not missing. In 1792, England sent Lord Macartney to the Chinese court, bearing costly presents and accompanied by a great retinue. But such an embassy could not register any success, beyond the result that England, also, henceforth stood in the list of the nations which had brought tribute to the emperor. The English embassy of Lord Amherst, about 1816, turned back without even having seen the throne of the dragons. Lord Amherst refused to kow-tow before the emperor of the Chinese. To throw himself down and to touch the ground with his brow, that, indeed, was asking too much from an upright Briton. Thus, no way to come to an understanding could be found. Trading continued to be conducted by barbarous methods.

The French and the English could not get along with each other at the time. Their sailors joined issue, in spite of the fact that the Chinese had given them separate islands to reside on; thus it could not be but that now and then a Chinese lost his life through their brawls. Chinese officials took drastic measures. In 1784, an English sailor who had killed a Chinese by mistake was strangled by order of a Chinese tribunal: life for life. In 1822, when the commander of the English frigate *Topaz* protected a compatriot with armed force against being handed over to Chinese jurisdiction, accused of double manslaughter, a regular battle took place. It was especially the obscure trade in opium which brought such things about. That trade was prohibited; but it flourished nevertheless. The East India Company, it is true, never imported opium itself. But it managed to turn over to the state, in England, one and a half million pounds sterling as its spoils. It encouraged, therefore, the culture of opium in India and liked to see the vessels of other nations taking the product to Canton and smuggling it, along the coasts, into the country. Relations between England and China became visibly strained; soon they must reach the goal of violence. Opium was already being smoked throughout China. The Chinese Emperor burst into tears when he became fully aware of this. "How can I die and appear before the shades of my ancestors till this evil has been wiped out!" thus he complained to his suite. The embargo of 1800 against opium was reinforced. A special commissary travelled from Peking to Canton, with the strictest orders either to abolish the opium trade or not to return alive.

Meanwhile the monopoly of the East India Company had come to an end. Henceforth (about 1834) an inspector of the British crown was to take over the supervision of English trade in Canton—a trade which was now free. The Chinese governor of Canton denied him official recognition. For three more years the trade in opium flourished. The Chinese commissary grew desperate; he used all means. Chinese officials suspected of smuggling opium were executed; their sons were debarred for life from all examinations prescribed by the state. Smokers were deprived, by the knife, of their upper lips, so that they could no longer hold the pipe. The commissary demanded the surrender of all the opium stored in foreign warehouses; at first without success. Then the governor of Canton ordered such Chinese as had been apprehended in trading opium, to be strangled below the American flag-pole within the factory. The foreigners rushed in; the mob took a hand; the inspector of the British crown demanded his passports. But the commissary held him till all the opium in Canton, six million dollars' worth of opium, had been surrendered.

That was the beginning of the opium war. The debate in the English parliament—where Sir George Staunton declared that it would be fatal to English power in India if such a blow against the prestige of the crown remained unpunished—ended with the resolution of an expedition against China.

In 1840 the British Fleet appeared before the seaport of Ting-Hai; the city of Ningpo was occupied;

Canton, Amoy, the river Yang-Tze and the river Teiho were blockaded.

The English met with a determined and courageous defence which, however, was impotent against modern weapons. Many high mandarins fell in battle; the soldiers held their posts, ready to come to a hand-to-hand fight till panic dispersed them, arising from the incomprehensible hail of iron.

Peace came in 1842, not before indescribable scenes had been enacted in the storming of Canton, Shanghai, Chin-Kiang. The terror, the abysmal shame of having been simply run down by these barbarians hit the Manchu officials profoundly. The despair at seeing the freedom of the great people sink away, under their high responsibility, at seeing the splendour and greatness of the Chinese Empire fade, drove them to suicide. They drowned their children in wells; they cut the throats of their women; behind locked doors whole families extinguished themselves. When the foreign men-of-war were anchored before Nanking, the emperor permitted his officials to treat for peace.

England made the following demands; and they were granted.

The cession of Hong Kong.

The opening-up of five trading ports: Amoy, Fu-

Cheu, Ningpo, Canton, Shanghai, to foreign trade and foreign settlement.

Twenty-one million dollars indemnity.

Fixing of a definite and exclusive tariff for foreign goods and Chinese exports.

Recognition of a direct, written intercourse, on an equal footing, between the officials of both sides.

In 1844, similar treaties were peacefully concluded with China by America and France; and later by other powers, Prussia among them.

Of the opium trade we read nothing in these treaties. The Chinese no longer tried to prevent it.

It is true that, in English bottoms, not only opium and cannon reached China. In 1807, Robert Morrison had come, the first protestant missionary at Canton. Later he became an interpreter for the East India Company; but his translations of Bible texts into the Chinese remained the foundation for subsequent protestant missions. It cannot be said that this gift of the Christian west has been nothing but a blessing for the Chinese. For these Bible texts had the misfortune of falling into the hands of a fanatic visionary of Canton, Hung Siutsuen by name, of the tribe of the Hakka. In an epileptic fit this man had seen a dragon, a tiger, and a cock, besides many people who invited him to enter a royal palanquin. Arrived at a resplendent palace, he was joyfully and enthusiastically received by the wise men and the saints of the nation. They purified him and then opened his body to take out heart and liver. These organs were replaced by fresh ones, red in colour; and at once the wound closed without leaving a scar. Thereupon the whole assembly repaired into another great hall of indescribable splendour where an old, bent-over man with a golden beard, draped in black garments, sat on a throne. Seeing Hung, he shed tears and said, "All creatures in the world owe me their existence. They wear my raiment and eat my bread; but not one has the heart to worship me. Woe to them! They take my gifts and sacrifice them to devils and demons. Go, and do not do as they do." With that he gave Hung a sword, a seal, and a yellow fruit. Hung took these tokens; and at once the assembly fell down before him as their master. Below, Hung saw the world. He saw corruption and crime. That sight was so terrible that he awoke. The illness lasted forty days. Often, in his dreams, there came to him a man who admonished him to fight against demons and devils. On his recovery, he became more and more convinced that he was called upon to rule over China and to win mighty wealth. It

35

came about that his wife's brother advised him to read the tracts of a certain Liang Afah, translations of Biblical passages. As he read, Hung became convinced that God the Father had appeared to him and that his guide, in his dream, had been Jesus Christ. "Had nobody ever sent me these books, then I might have doubted the truth of my visions; now I am certain that I was called."

His power to transfer, with demonic conviction, upon those who surrounded him, the belief in the Bible as the foundation and credential of his mission gathered followers about him. The miraculous nature of the Mosaic creation, of the downfall of Sodom and Gomorrha, or of the last judgment, presented with real seriousness and a deep, moral power, attracted strangers to him. Some believed and were baptised in a near-by brook. Others came to debate. All followed him to subdue the country with fire and sword. For fifteen years the empire, in the sign of the mission of King Tsuen, was devastated, from Canton north to the Hoang-Ho. Twenty million people lost their lives through this strange conversion. Not till the foreigners helped, and precisely through the genius of a real Christian, through General Gordon who commanded the imperial troops, was King Tsuen defeated. When, deserted by his faithful, the prophet had perished in his own palace, the imperial obituary said of him, "Words cannot convey an idea of the misery and the destruction which he has caused; the measure was full, and the wrath of God and man had risen against him."

The foreigners helped the imperial government to choke this Taiping rebellion. But, in this great danger of the imperial power, they did not forget their own interests. About 1854, in the midst of civil war, the envoys of England, America, and France obtained from the imperial provost of Shanghai that control over the levy of Chinese duties which they still hold today. That was a plain encroachment upon the internal administration of China of which we shall hear a good deal more.

An unbroken sequence of violent inroads on the part of all Christian nations—inroads which opened the empire up to the foreigners—accompanied by rebellion and apostasy in the interior, followed that year 1854 beyond the last days of the century. Urged on by the lack of restraint on the part of numerous foreign envoys, the Chinese government nevertheless resisted like a wall. That government demanded reverence for the Son of Heaven and that religious reserve before the ruler of the Celestial Empire which had lived for millennia, within the people, as a storied past and a sacred tradition. In the life of the people, this moral demand remained a power which could not but give victory to the army, with such a helper on its side. That which was civically good and which fearlessly held on to what was right, must, in the idea of the Chinese people, ultimately prevail even over armed might. In this belief nation and government were at one as far as their attitude to the foreigner was concerned. But the more the actions of nation and government conformed to this, their own conviction and to what they considered right, the more they laid themselves open to attack by the foreigner; the more did they lose.

Not from petty selfishness, not from racial hate did the Chinese defend themselves against the foreigners, but from a haughty aversion, nourished through the spirit of a culture five millennia old.

This spirit of the people we can firstly interpret by the old Chinese language. A runic, written language rises before us, handed down through millennia; the language in which Confucius proclaimed Chinese wisdom five hundred years before Christ. This written language could only be read; as a spoken language it had become incomprehensible many centuries ago. In the later China, as life was lived, a new spoken language arose; new written symbols, not displacing the old ones, had been superadded to the innovations of the workaday world. In spite of that, through all the external changes, the spirit of the people remained the same; and the traditional language, the so-called language of the mandarins, remained the language of literature and of bureaucracy. In the schools, the village school as well as the university, the old tokens remained the language of instruction to the most modern time.

With the acquisition of this old language the circle of life closed in upon the mind of the child. The child was received within the wizardry of wisdom, within the spell of the sacred signs.

> "The best that is in man responds
>   At first to man;
>   Till earthy urgings cut these bonds."

Such are the first words of the "Book of the Three Signs"—the first words of the Chinese primer. First the children learned their primer by heart without understanding its meaning. As instruction advanced, there followed an explanation of the words and an interpretation of their meaning. The formal beauty of the style was appreciated; the significance for life explained.

As Christ taught his congregation in church and synagogue, thus the church of the Chinese was the school of Confucius. What is needed for moral life, what lends existence an aim beyond itself, all that, besides art and poetry, the master embraced in his doctrine. What he who knows should explore and grasp and search for and what he should not search for—it was all contained in the ever open shrine of the Confucian books. Ethic wisdom, right conduct, dignity in human life; the order of the state, right duty of ruler and citizen, in war and in peace, that is what they taught to the understanding of childhood as well as of old age. School, church, and state; these three were embraced by the "Book of Books": the book of the precepts and the sayings of Confucius.

This book furnished every Chinese with his intellectual, moral, and even æsthetic panoply. It bred aristocratic men.

For the people it was a manual of instruction, constitution, and revelation; an eternal, august monument. Its tradition circulated in proverb, in use-and-wont, in all things of the day as "the spirit which is the main thing even for the material interests."

What a textbook which crowns learning with the charm of the perfection of wisdom! "What a heart-felt joy it is," says Confucius, "to acquire knowledge and to translate that knowledge, by acquiring it, into action."

But the "Book of Books" is no book of formulas. Once, when the subject was a famous piece of music, Confucius remarked, "It has all the excellence of physical harmony. It also has the perfection of moral greatness." Moral greatness consisted for him in devotion of the soul, love of truth, and knowledge acquired by learning. But the essence of existence consisted for him in the order of Heaven. "Who violates the order of Heaven, he has nothing left to which to pray." Has western religion ever expressed the shadow of god-forsakenness with similar delicacy and power? When all men possess these things and honour them, then "is the empire in the state of blessed peace."

The things which disquiet the physical harmony of existence, anxious questionings after a beyond and a ghostly existence, the master declined to deal with.

41

Not such things is man to explore. Perfection of *this* life, there is his world; there the goal of his striving. Art, too, is a striving in that direction. A disciple asked for the canon of art. Confucius replied, "That is a difficult question. But in art, as in use-and-wont, it is better to be simple-minded than to be ingenious. In the sacrifice for the dead, soul-shaken mourning counts for more than painstaking formality; and in painting, ornamentation and colouring are of the second order compared with the design." "Then," the disciple observed, "art itself is of the second order?" "My friend, you have said it. Now I can discourse with thee on poetry."

Since the book appeals to thought, it has withstood the change of the millennia. Generations have come and gone; the picture of the universe has changed before their eyes. But every age has found truth in the book. It deals with the eternal, unchangeable essence of earthly existence. We, too, look into the world with eyes different from those of, let me say, Angelus Silesius; but has that changed the essence of truth? "The moral life of man consists in loving men." That is part and parcel of the essence of all life on earth. A disciple said, "What I do not wish that others should do to me, that I should not wish to do to others." "Yes," said Confucius, "but thou hast not reached that point." Another asked, "To be poor yet not subservient; to be rich and yet not arrogant, what is to be thought of that?" "It is good," judged the master; "but it is better to be poor and yet content; to be rich and yet considerate." "I understand," said the disciple; "we are to cut and to grind, to carve and to file." "I see," replied Confucius, "thou knowest how to apply the moral. The wise man searches for what he needs within himself. Only a fool seeks it in others. When it is a question of morals, no teacher is needed."

Such teaching breeds aristocratic men! And thus the sayings and conversations of Confucius revealed to the Chinese people the ethical maxims of life, of the struggle for righteousness and dignity in the existence of man. The consequence of this spirit was for the Chinese people that it had a culture of considerateness. A culture of the protection of the poor by the rich and of the weak by the strong; that it possessed a family consciousness extending to the remotest members and a society led by a strong feeling for natural justice. The feeling for responsibility was deeply rooted in the Chinese.

There has probably never been a foreigner in China who has not lived to see an example of what this moral

constitution of the Chinese people amounted to. The
merchant needed no written agreement with his
Chinese correspondent. The stranger could trust the
least among the Chinese. Whoever, travelling in the
interior, arrived at the end of rail or of navigation,
surrendered his whole baggage to entirely unknown
coolies. They took it for whole days through the country, left to themselves, and finally reported with not
a needle missing. They had this feeling of responsibility. Yet these coolies are poor. A single piece of
baggage, belonging to such a stranger, would have
made the bearer rich. Such a coolie, in the evening
after a long day of travel, will turn back for many
hours of walking in order to buy the well-earned rice
of his supper for a penny less.

Under such a constitution China needed no further
public opinion in order to regulate matters of state.
The magistrate under whose jurisdiction frequent
crimes were committed, was punished by the emperor.
Somebody asked Confucius why he took no active
part in the government of the country. He answered
by the counter question, "What are the duties of a
good son? To obey his parents; and to be a brother
to his brother. Let everyone do his duty in the family;
for that, too, is a task of government. But if that is a

task of government why should anyone then take an active part in the government of the country in order to do his duty by the government?"

Confucius named three major maxims for the government of a country:

To see to it that there is enough food for the whole people.

To see to it that there is a good army.

To see to it that the people put its trust in the rulers.

Thereupon a disciple asked which of these maxims could best be spared. "Disband the army," said the reply; "and next, dispense with the provision for food. Old people, it is true, will die of hunger; but without the confidence of the people in its rulers there can be no government of any kind."

For this reason, then, the Chinese had neither a public opinion which bore strongly upon matters of state nor a good army. They had no considerable carrying trade because Confucius had taken no interest in trade, industry, and technical achievements. These domains were not included within the circle of Confucian wisdom. They did not belong to the things essential for the life of the Chinese; they were left to the workaday world. That is the reason why ancient

China has never developed the exact sciences, algebra and geometry, physics and chemistry; nor steam navigation, though they had known the compass for millennia.

This whole trend did not suit the Europeans.

Backward China must not remain in its self-contentment, its self-glorification! Europe represented "the progress of mankind"; and, fired by this conviction, driven by the materialistic spirit of the people and an aggressive colonial policy, the public opinion of Europe, and above all, of England, decided that China must surrender herself to the freedom of travel and trade. Preparations were made to take the measure of China with larger cannon, England leading all. Other western nations followed with similar achievements, till, by the end of the century, the whole Christian world rolled with the drum-beat of western felicity.

Was this great nation "backward"—as people said to comfort themselves—this nation whose greatest mind had hung up the "word" over the head of every one of its members, like a sword of Damocles and like a star? Had not Confucius taught, "That is the thing which the wise man and the good man dreads, to die without having made the people happy?"

46

History shows us a never resting, always reformatory progress of Chinese science; of a search, on the part of the Chinese spirit, after the essence of truth. Look at the precious things which the foreigner fetched from the shops of Chinese artisan or artist: at Dresden, Berlin, London, New York, and Paris there are huge collections of treasures of Chinese art; and we write thick-bellied tomes about them. From the soil of China, tilled for many thousand years, the peasant still takes undiminished crops. True enough, industry and mass production, machine guns and poison-gas remained unknown.

What the spirit of the Chinese people had achieved was something else: this, that a numberless people, by virtue of strict morals and conscious restraint had outlasted five millennia; and this people is even today, mentally and physically, a vital branch of mankind, full of sap. A proud people.

True, when the Europeans arrived, it was visited by the devastations of epidemics, floods and famines; but nevertheless contented and peacefully contemplative. The Chinese had no need for, nor knowledge of, the blessings of machine and sport; they did not want to know of the only true philosophy of life, that of action. That philosophy they did not consider "fair";

47

and they looked down upon the super-man of Nietzsche who, in overweening fullness of strength, free from a weakly consideration for the herd of average men, is allowed to unfold, and to erect into a general law of life, his natural "will-to-power."

Europe, however, went on its way. How many things could not the western man bring home! Now by warlike raids, now by treaties, western nations robbed old China of colonies or concessions. Their materialistic spirit urged them on to explode the spirit of China. They settled in modern cities in China and erected there a system of living and trading independent of the rest of the country, under western law, with an administration and a police of their own. They sent traders and missionaries into the very heart of the country. They succeeded in cutting up the land by railways, post-office systems, and telegraph lines. All these institutions they founded, free from any weakly consideration for the native spirit and, I am sorry to say, often without any consideration for the suzerainty of the Chinese people.

And what did the Chinese do against that? They did what they could. But against the will-to-power, erected into a law of life, this China which relied on moral powers could do but little.

There was Chang Chitung, a viceroy, who, to save the country, wanted to adopt the very methods of the interloper. He erected an arsenal, founded a number of industries—to learn that the machine is nothing, that the spirit of the machine is everything. The Chinese lacked that spirit which values action as such. They lacked the matter-of-fact devotion to the machine, to industry as a measure of human value. Machines and industrial equipment decayed; and today the ruins lie scattered at Wu-Chang and Han-Yang along the banks of the Yang-Tze-Kiang. There was an imperial court which bought foreign arms and men-of-war and delegated Prince Yung Lu and Viceroy Li Hung Chang to create a modern army. The army was beaten by Japan. The court lost Korea and Formosa to the Japanese. The same imperial court, advised by its highest dignitaries, in a patriotic but short-sighted way, connived at the fanatic Boxer rebellion against the foreign embassies at Peking. The Empress-Regent, in 1900, still believed that, with the destruction of the embassies, the foreign powers would be defeated. Before the united expeditionary forces of the foreign powers the court had to flee from the capital; the palaces of the forbidden city were looted by the foreign soldiery. The country was only the more deeply involved in indemnities, the more deeply bowed under foreign control. At last the dynasty fell itself. The confidence of the people in its rulers was lost; the year of 1911 brought the revolution and the republic.

But the attempt to create, within the spirit of the people, the necessary conditions for self-assertion by means of a political revolution—that attempt failed. Even for the mere outward form of government, the chief thing is the spirit of the people which is to live under it; it is never possible to change that spirit by a political reorganisation. And the spirit is the ultimate reality of the people.

Meanwhile, the "progress of mankind" slipped into the World War. For four years, the strong public opinion and the materialistic spirit of the Christian nations battled before the astonished eyes of the Chinese. China discovered that even the closed front of the foreign will-to-power disintegrated at last. Before the eyes of the Chinese, the arrogant conceit of the Christian-capitalistic world—the conceit that they represented the "progress of mankind" because they had the largest cannon—stood unveiled.

And already another Asiatic people, in furious revolt, shook off the will-to-power-over-others of those capitalistic nations. The Russians rose and planted, for the economically weaker nations, the banner of self-determination; to go their own way henceforth.

The Chinese were learning.

A change of spirit began to prepare itself. Those convulsions and spasms which leaders and followers had undergone, up to the time of the revolution of 1911, the struggle of the intellectual forces of the country with western ideas and their effects, had not remained without result. Thinkers and patriots tore loose from tradition; from school and church of Confucius; and they demanded the same of the people. They attacked the old language, the classical style. They preached zealously against the chaining of the spirit of youth by tradition. Out of the circle of ideas of the living present they created a new literature in the living language of the day. By decree of state, the old, classical books were banned from elementary instruction and relegated to the universities. The result is that the mental bond of Confucius by which the unfolding mind had been circled lies torn. Youth has the right and the linguistic arsenal to discuss without restraint the problems of the time, of politics and economics.

Thus there arose an urging, struggling public

opinion, led by the grown-up youth of the country, fed by the growing youth, by students and scholars. Boys of the middle school, fourteen years old, debated politics and economics; girls took part in demonstrative processions. Irresistibly speaks this public opinion. First of all it aims at nothing less than the driving-out of foreign dominion. The paralysis consequent to the influence of foreign tenets upon the development of a native culture is being overcome in the schools.

Such is the new spirit of the people which is spreading. For this spirit Sun Yatsen became the leader. From Canton the revolt sweeps over the country, stirs up the minds of the people against that which is handed down and against any sort of will-to-power over the cultural, political, or economic self-determination of the Chinese. Can anyone, in view of this abysmally foaming stream, still believe that it can be stemmed before it has reached the utmost limits of the Chinese nation, within or without the Chinese wall, and in the colonies as well? Doubt is still being voiced whether really all China can be involved in the nationalistic movement. The possibility of a division of the empire into north and south is still being discussed: the possibility of an assertion of the racial

CHIANG KAISHEK

Commander-in-chief of the Nationalist Army

A PROCESSION OF NATIONALIST PROPAGANDISTS

difference between Cantonese and the Chinese of the north. The opinion is heard that finally perhaps the Confucian spirit may yet resume its mastery over the innovations.

That the Confucian spirit will live on in the customs and usages of the people is a certainty. That Confucian morals and ethics will prevail in conduct, we must heartily hope and wish. But that the spiritual revolt already embraces the Chinese people as a whole, that is the very thing which gives it its irresistible power from which events shoot up in spite of all politics. That the nationalist movement started from Canton is mere chance. It is a national wave which might have started anywhere—*wherever Sun Yatsen was at work.*

Perhaps the maxim of Wilhelm Roscher stands now sufficiently relieved against this background of principles to make it clear that all sides of the utterance of the Chinese people need to be conscientiously considered and respected if we want to understand present events scientifically. The political utterance of the Chinese—those events in China which are pointed against the foreigners—represent only a single arrow from the quiver. As Russia did in 1917, China has begun to create for itself a sphere of existence of its own. Both nations have initiated an era of their own; and—a significant thing—both nations, in doing so, have found each other.

This meeting of the two nations, of Russians and Chinese, is, after all, not a mere political manœuvre. As such, representatives of the economic-political press bureaus would like to paint it. Were it no more than that, the position of the foreign powers in China, above all of England, would not seem so helpless as it does. A stronger thing which they have in common binds China and Russia together. What unites them is the common revolt against the will-to-power, erected into a law of life, of capitalistic-industrial society. Russia revolted against the will-to-power over the workers' class; China revolts against the will-to-power over the cultural, economic, and political existence of the whole nation. This stronger community which underlies all political events impedes, in the last resort, all the political and military resolutions of the western powers which have a capitalistic organisation, including Japan and America. In China, no separate groups of powers which otherwise stand on the same plane of culture—as was the case in the World War —face each other; facing each other stand two groups of nations which strive to express themselves on

THE PEARL: BY WAY OF INTRODUCTION

different planes of cultural endeavour. Political and economic interests stand between them as the grain lies between the millstones. For the powers with a capitalistic organisation, above all England, the grist is the indispensable colonial interest on the continent of Asia. For China and Russia, it is the announcement of their individual claims to an existence in the world and the right entitling them to their own philosophy of life.

In the colonies and concessions of the foreigners in China, foreigners and Chinese live side by side; to every foreigner there are a hundred Chinese. This ratio holds good for the British colony of Hong Kong as well as for Singapore. At all these places these Chinese, having as they do a public opinion, represent a corresponding danger to British colonial possessions. What is England doing about it? We may rest assured that England does what she can.

First of all England changed the international settlement of Shanghai—not without the co-operation of other world powers, including Japan and America—into a military and naval base; in the east of China she conducts a systematic propaganda; the newspaper forest resounds with the violated rights of man, English rights, of course; with atrocities committed by the Chinese against the foreign benefactors. Nor must it be forgotten that even in Indo-China there live Chinese. In Manchuria, indispensable to Japan, there live Chinese. In black letters on a flaming wall the revolt of the whole of Asia is proclaimed.

The isolation of Germany by the Entente cost King Edward VII a whole decade or more. How long it will take present-day England to close the circle of the powers with a capitalistic organisation for the war of defence against the Asiatic violation of the sacred will-to-power over the Asiatics, we do not know. But that such is the determined policy of England is evident enough.

If the last war was called the World War, what are we going to call this war in which really two worlds of opposite orbits will collide?

Meanwhile England stands guard over the public opinion of western nations and states. There is nothing petty about her. Even a certain German engineer is being watched. To be a friend of Chinese nationalist leaders, is to be suspected of a knowledge of the truth; yes, of a desire to speak that truth. For England, however, truth is a precious pearl which she means to guard well indeed.

I. THE DOWNFALL OF THE MANCHU DYNASTY

It was in March 1925. The telegraph spread the news of the death of Sun Yatsen throughout the world. Many Chinese, not without anxiety in their expression, said, "The greatest man of our country is dead!"

This verdict could not be expected to find universal endorsement. Innumerable people were then and still are too profoundly affected by the work of the great man. His figure still looms too close to permit of a long view into the future.—How should we contemporaries know who, within our own decades, has greatly lived and done? To have been the president of a great country does not mean that the incumbent of such an office has been a great man. Have Roosevelt or Wilson been great men? Does the financial power of the great men of our exchanges stamp the latter into eminent figures of our time?

The Russians glorify Lenin like a saint. To uncounted millions he is the essence of all that is contemptible.

But the traveller who stands before the tomb of Lenin understands the belief of the new Russia. He understands that the holy city of Moscow has received within that austere building behind which the golden towers of the Kremlin shine, a new saint, a sombre saint, but yet a *saint*. For he has much suffered for his people, he has fought for the poor man in the street and won his heart for evermore.

Our present time likes to look up to men of great material achievements in industry, production, or economics. With all its reverence it cannot make these idols of the day into great men.

Even in our realistic world the great man is made great by the idea alone. Only a spiritual man who, in life-long devotion to the idea and in unconditional self-sacrifice, delivers the laden millions, in spite of the rulers—only he is the great man to a nation. It is necessary to stand in the midst of the Russian peasantry in order to realize, in the free self-reliance of the mujik, the effect of that idea which Lenin implanted by his suffering and his struggling; with the same mujik whose nauseating servile spirit under Czardom once drew upon him the contempt and the pity of western Europe. The change is unheard-of. Whoever has recognised this liberation of the human consciousness, with the enormous possibilities of its effects, understands that, to the Russians, Lenin is a saint. For all times he will remain, within the life and the work of the Russian people, a truly great man. It is beside the point when western Europeans occasionally object that, with all their rebellion and their bloodshed, the Russians gained no more than our own peasantry and our own workmen have enjoyed long ago and won peacefully. To the Russian, the new-won freedom to develop himself is no less revolutionary for the reason that other nations have held this freedom before. To the Russian, the revolution was the gateway into new life within his ethnic, social, and moral development.

It is that which we must keep before our eyes when we hear the Chinese say that the country has lost with Sun Yatsen its greatest man and leader. Only from out of the midst of the present popular movement can we understand the verdict of the Chinese which is almost equivalent to a consecration. The ideas of Sun Yatsen bestowed upon his people the power to soar into orbits which promise a greater happiness. History will judge his work. But even an enemy dare not call him anything but a great-hearted, faithful, truthful character. That idea which he kindled within his people into a mighty flame glowed in himself. In every action of his life he remained faithful to it.

Born 1866, in the province of Kwang-Tung, he grew up in a family which belonged to the lower middle-class. As a boy, he whetted his thought by means of the doctrine contained in the Confucian books; and he developed his memory by learning the numberless symbols of the written language. He escaped from this old school of every Chinese boy only in order to pick up, within a foreign lyceum, the scent of the mysteries of western culture in English word-lists, in arithmetic, and algebra. The classical books of Confucius and Mencius, in which every scholar of the middle school in China is instructed, initiated him into the foundation of Chinese wisdom. That wisdom is equivalent to Chinese political economy. For in the history of Chinese antiquity good and evil are distinguished by the canon of the welfare or the suffering of the Chinese people. We must not, then, marvel at the fact that young Sun Yatsen connected the whole newly-acquired western knowledge with the political and economic condition of his country and his people. While, at the foreign university of Hong

Kong, he studied medicine, his whole thought and search was for the changes, for better or worse, which the foreign culture of the West would bring about in the condition of his people. Foreign industrial methods, in the name of which foreign culture demanded entrance everywhere at the gates of China, became more and more impetuous in their desire to make China happy. The young scientist watched tensely for the course which the imperial government of the Manchus was going to pursue with regard to the invasion of foreign ways. With suppressed eagerness he observed the effects of the foreign institutions; how the postal service, the telegraph, the railways, and the newspapers, by abolishing the distances between the provinces, opposed to the already sickening rulership of the Manchus a solid and dangerous power. It is easy to understand the glowing desire of the young Sun Yatsen to free his country and people, by means of western science and technique, of the devastating epidemics of the plague, of the chronic famines, and the periodical floods which covered whole provinces. The passion for this gigantic work of reform never left him throughout his life. Nothing is more pleasing to watch than the anger of this true, young spirit at the rotten and decaying authority of

61

the Manchus. They accepted the annihilation of millions of their subjects, recurring with a horrible regularity, as a judgment of God. They had never the strength to understand the new things, nor the courage to oppose them honestly. To throw down this impotent rule, in order to make room for a democratic government of the people—in that Sun Yatsen recognised the task of his life. In 1892, he had taken his degree in medicine at Hong Kong. He had absorbed foreign science and the idea of the freedom of the people as well as the English tradition—that tradition of the English school which speaks of the responsibility for the uplifting of backward nations and on which England bases her colonial policies. Sun Yatsen believed that, with the downfall of the Manchu dynasty, a gate would be opened through which his people could enter freedom. The attraction of his personality soon gathered similarly-bent minds and hearts about him from southern China, in an association for "the renovation of China." He became its leader in propaganda and literature. The activities of this fiery head did not remain hidden from the imperial government. The secret societies which were formed in Kwang-Tung, were discovered; and the Tartar general of Canton knew how cruelly to frus-

trate, in 1895, an attempt at revolution which had for
its object to occupy city and province. Out of sixteen
leaders, fifteen were executed. Sun Yatsen was the
only one to escape. There followed years of persecution; and when a prize was placed upon his head, he
withdrew from his enemies by a flight to England.
Always trying to win followers for his life-work, he
strayed through England and America. Especially
in the latter, he kindled the republican fire among the
Chinese who lived abroad. He gained friends, but was
ever pursued by the secret agents of the imperial embassies of China.

Yet, even within the empire, the seed sown
sprouted. Secret societies multiplied and extended
even over the northern provinces. The never-ceasing
insistence of the foreign embassies on innovations in
the empire acted like yeast in the attempts of Chang
Chitung and of Li Hung Chang, vice-roy of Chili,
creating vacua. The foreigners did not understand
what was going on below the surface; consideration
for the spirit of the people was unknown to them.
When, in 1898, the young emperor Kuang Hsu called
the great reformer K'ang Yuwei and his spiritual
confederate Liang Chichao and others into the council of state, they thought their kingdom of heaven had

come in China. But the dream lasted only for a hundred days. Yuan Shikai betrayed the plans of the young emperor to the Manchu reactionaries at the court. These gathered about the Empress-Regent Tzu Hsi; the young emperor was sent into the exile of an island within the Forbidden City; and the Empress-Regent annulled all decrees of reform. That the young emperor did not have to die at once, he owed to the protests of the foreign embassies at Peking. But this meddling with the innermost affairs of the dynasty served only to increase the anger of the Manchu circles against the foreigners. Indignation led the Manchu rulers to those fanatical mistakes which ended, in 1900, with the Boxer revolt. The young emperor had to die anyway. He had to die one day before the Empress-Regent.

The deposition of the reform emperor fatally widened the breach between the Chinese and their Manchu rulers. From the security of the foreign settlements, the secret societies hurled now the gravest accusations against the Manchus. Chinese newspapers in Shanghai accused the regents of the intention to wipe out the influence, accumulated through centuries, of Chinese officials on the government. Chinese viceroys saw their offices threatened. Chang Chitung is said to have deserted the young emperor and his reform movement in order to curry favour with the Empress-Regent. But perhaps it was his recognition of the fact that the road he had taken lost itself in futility; perhaps even self-defence. Chang Chitung was Chinese; he was concerned about the existence of the Chinese. Now the secret societies advanced against the viceroys of the provinces. Yet, a new attempt at revolution, led by Sun Yatsen in Canton, in 1900, again remained without success. There is, however, a document, in the possession of the present minister of the nationalist government, Eugene Chen, dated 1903, which, above eighteen signatures of viceroys and governors, appoints Sun Yatsen president of a republic to be founded.

The ways of popular policies are obscure; their course was lighted up for the foreigners by no star of insight. Even after February 12, 1912, the date of the public abdication of the Manchu Regent, the foreigners in China believed that the proclamation of a republic was the result of chance. To prove that, the English historian J. O. P. Bland filled many pages of his book on the revolution. The foreigners saw nothing but what they could attribute to their own influence on the Manchu government. They saw nothing but the reform movements promoted, after the Japanese war and after the suppression of the Boxer revolt, by the Empress-Regent Tzu Hsi, and later by the Regent during the minority of the imperial child Hsuan Tung. They promised themselves a good deal from the decree of August 27, 1908, which gave a commission nine years' time within which to prepare a constitutional Manchu monarchy. It was known that a parliament could be brought together only from among the officials and the loyal middle class; in other words, that the very circles in which the foreigners pursued their trade would be strengthened. Such a direction could be approved of and desired for China. But the intelligentzia of China was not satisfied with that. In October 1911, there broke out, in Wu-Chang, with the co-operation of the regiments of Colonel Li Yuan-Hung, and at the same time in Canton, an open revolt of the secret societies Tung Meng Hui and Kao Lao Hui. About Christmas 1911, Sun Yatsen returned from exile to Shanghai; and on January 1, 1912, he entered Nanking as elected president of the newly-proclaimed republic.

The foreign powers did not like to see this development of things. But for their materialistic spirit it proved too strong.

It must be true, as J. O. P. Bland writes, that the foreigners did not believe in the clear intention and determination of Young China to establish a republican form of government. For they might have saved the imperial court of which they now quite approved. In the hour of the crisis the imperial court sent for Yuan Shikai. Since the death of the Empress-Regent Tzu Hsi this man had had to spend his hours in the retirement of the country. After the change in the incumbency of the throne he had been removed from the imperial council, on account of his former treachery to Emperor Kuang Hsu. On October 27, 1911, he was entrusted by the emperor with the suppression of the revolt in Wu-Chang; on November 8, he was appointed chancellor of the empire. That Yuan Shikai had, in the imperial council of the Empress-Regent Tzu Hsi, spoken for a constitutional monarchy, was well known. He was acceptable to the foreign powers. The military situation in Wu-Chang was not hopeless for the imperial court. Indeed, the imperial troops had taken the positions of the revolutionaries on the Hankau bank of the Yang-Tze-Kiang; with their Krupp guns they commanded the situation. The foreign embassies had promised Yuan Shikai that the political and financial "four-power-syndicate" would be at his disposal with large sums. A loan to the imperial government of six million pound sterling was being mooted.

Under such auspices Yuan Shikai entered, on November 12, 1911, into negotiations with the revolutionaries. They were to be satisfied with the immediate declaration of a constitutional Manchu monarchy. Li Yuang-Hung was a confidant of Yuan Shikai. Followers of Sun Yatsen, however, the later Kuo-Mintang, had meanwhile made themselves masters of the Chinese city of Shanghai, as also of the cities of Su-Cheu and Hang-Chow; and a republican committee had been put in power in Shanghai, under the leadership of Wu Tingfang. This committee insisted on the proclamation of a republic. On December 11, 1911, Wu Tingfang went so far as to threaten that further negotiations between envoys of Yuan Shikai (Tang Shaoyi) and Li Yuang-Hung would not be recognised. This energetic conduct had such an immediate success that the foreign offices of the western nations grew afraid with regard to a loan to the imperial government. Yes, political complications arose in connection with the international loan to China. Japan and Russia refused to stand aside while England, France, Germany, and America took steps to divide among them the financing of China. The consequence was that the loan to Yuan Shikai did not come off. Yuan Shikai, who had had the offer, from Shanghai, of the presidency of the republic, decided to make common cause with the revolutionaries. On his part, now, he urged the imperial regent to abdicate, that being the only way to avoid bloodshed and to preserve the peace of the country.

Sun Yatsen had nothing else in view but the peace of the country. His was an unselfish and naïvely trustful character. That prevented him from ever thinking anything but that those who surrounded him and came near him were guided by the same unselfishness and honesty of purpose as he himself. In the proclamation of the republic he saw no more than the first step towards the embodiment of the idea which his people would create. The gateway into freedom had been opened. The blessings that were bound to come were to fall to the share of a unified empire. He persuaded the national convention into which the republican committee of the Kuo-Mintang had meanwhile widened out, to elect Yuan Shikai president. It had indeed been due to the sums sent to him by his friends overseas and to the arms which his business relations in Japan had procured for him that the revolution had been brought about. But Yuan Shikai could, against that much, place the organised resources of the whole north; he enjoyed the good-will of the foreign embassies. If it were possible to graft upon the central organisations of the empire a republican representation of the people, then it might be possible to avoid steeping the empire, through the republic, into an initial confusion. On February 14, 1912, an invitation was issued to Yuan Shikai to come to Nanking in order to be inaugurated as president. On February 15 Sun Yatsen abdicated. He wished henceforth to devote himself to the better part of his mission, to the development of the natural resources of the country, to the building of arteries of traffic, to the prevention of famines, to the opium problem, and similar things.

But because a great mind wants to wrestle, within the house, with everything that is amiss, the wolves do not shed their pelt in the bush. The arch-enemy of political innovation is not the representative strength of the system that is being fought. It stands, visible to all, a target for the arrows of a just cause—to be hit. The evil enemy is the caste of a system that has taken root under the protection of the old power. Those who were converted by their interest; those who, when the battle is fought, overrun like ants the new edifice and calling themselves "sane moderation," weighting down the new thing so it cannot sweep clean, and who impede it to the profit of their selfishness: such are the arch-enemies of great renovation. Soon Sun Yatsen had to learn it. Yuan Shikai and his followers were of that type. The new president used a mutiny of the troops at Peking as a pretext in order to stay away from Nanking; and the formal inauguration of the president took place, on March 10, 1912, at Peking. That was the first great disappointment of the revolutionaries of Nanking; their intention to move the capital to Nanking had been thwarted.

The foreign powers finally kept their promises; they helped Yuan Shikai. They assisted with the troops of their embassies in suppressing the military mutiny; they advanced money on a loan which was being negotiated with Tang Shaoyi, the chancellor of Yuan Shikai. They did not help Sun Yatsen who had been counting on the assistance of a loan, on the part of the political and financial syndicate of powers, for his economic plans for the betterment of the conditions of his people. His experiences did away with any illusion with regard to the "peaceful penetration" of

China, by the foreigners, with banks and railways. Nothing remained of the tradition of the English school according to which the foreigners conducted their colonial policies from a "feeling of responsibility" for the backward nations of Asia. It was at this time that he wrote his indictment of the *"Imperialistic Rule"* of the foreigners in China.

The history of the politico-financial syndicate of powers for the peaceful penetration of China is a mere repetition of the chapter on the opening of China for foreign trade and traffic. The beginnings reach back into the time when the hunt was on for railway concessions. In 1895, the English Banking Corporation of Hong Kong and Shanghai had made an agreement with the German-Asiatic Bank to eliminate competition. Whenever one of the two parties acquired a concession, both were to benefit jointly. In 1898, England secured, by means of diplomatic pressure, the exclusive right to build five railways in the Yang-Tze valley. This concession was transferred to the Banking Corporation of Hong Kong and Shanghai. Before the year expired, this corporation merged itself with the French Bank under the title "Chinese Central Railway, Ltd.," in order to finance jointly certain railways north of the

Yang-Tze-Kiang. Germany secured for itself, in the peace treaty of Kiao-Chow, the exclusive right to finance and to build railways in the province of Shan-Tung. In the same year Japan acquired a privileged position in the province of Fu-Kien; France, in parts of the province of Yun-Nan. Thus the Great Policy of the foreign powers was inaugurated to secure for each of them a financial position of power; China had been divided into "spheres of interest." Yet, even so, the foreign interests were incompatible. When, in 1909, England prepared to make use of her exclusive rights in the Yang-Tze valley, Germany claimed her share, basing her claim on the agreement of the banks arrived at in 1895. America also spoke up. By means of a personal protest of President Taft, addressed to the Chinese emperor, America also received a share in these railway enterprises. Thus the "four-power syndicate"—England, France, Germany, and the United States—became the dominant financial power in China. Yet even Russia had, in 1896 and 1898, wrested a sphere of interest and an exclusive right to finance railways in Manchuria from China. In 1899, England had entered with Russia into a mutual agreement by which neither should disturb the other within her sphere of interest. As a consequence of the Russo-Japanese war, however, the privileges which Russia had acquired in Manchuria fell to Japan. When, then, in 1911, the four-power syndicate prepared to save the Manchu dynasty, thereby securing a decisive influence within the empire, Japan and Russia had protested. From considerations of international policy, they were received within the syndicate of the powers. It is not to be marvelled at that the experiences of Sun Yatsen led him to pass a verdict on this syndicate which was altogether condemnatory. That high idealism in which he had promised himself every assistance, on the part of the powers, in the task of bettering the conditions of his people, proved to be no more than a pious illusion. The powers had their spheres of interest and their mutual agreements; and nothing else mattered. They were realists. A newly founded republic demanded unconditional freedom in disposing of the loans. The powers insisted upon control of the loans. Thus the question whether the republic or the foreign financial powers were to have the power of the purse in China remained unsolved.

Slowly but with deadly certainty, meanwhile, the broad mass of the official caste rolled along, to cover up the rent with which the revolution had torn conventions and to fill it up. The national assembly at Nanking had decreed the institution of a provisional national council. It was to consist of five delegates from each of the provincial assemblies which had met in obedience to the decree of August 27, 1908; and it was to take measures for a general election for a national convention. This national convention, to consist of a senate and a house of deputies, was conceived as the legislative body of the republic. Accordingly, Yuan Shikai took such steps among the Tutus (governors) of the provinces as were in order. The provisional national council met on April 29, 1912, at Peking. The representatives of the Kuo-Mintang at once became aware of the success of Yuan Shikai's work; in this, that they found themselves face to face with a firm opposition. Behind that opposition, president and cabinet were safely entrenched. The great national reforms of the republicans of Nanking went down in the struggle of the parties. When, in April 1913, the constitutional national convention assembled, it appeared that the old henchmen of the government had succeeded in "buying in" their parties. The majority consisted of the reactionary middle class and of such as followed the leading personalities of the old system. Treacherous murder did

away with Sung Chiao-Yen, the leader of the Kuo-
Mintang deputies when he entrained at Shanghai for
Peking. Nobody could any longer talk of a representation of the people in the sense of the Kuo-Mintang. The people called the national convention nothing but "a collection of silk frocks."

In the Yang-Tze valley there followed at once a
new attempt at revolution, on the part of the Kuo-
Mintang; but the revolt was quickly suppressed by
Yuan Shikai. Once more Sun Yatsen went into exile
to Japan.

Thus fell the proud aims.

The old system had lost its legitimate master. It
had received the name of a republic. But the rule of
the mandarins scrambled across the filled-in rent and
continued to flourish. Yuan Shikai was "the strong
man" for whom reaction always cries at such times;
as such he enjoyed the confidence of the foreign
powers. He was granted and, without asking the national convention, accepted the loan of the syndicate
of powers. The Kuo-Mintang raved about it in the
national convention. But our "strong man" went on
his way. The ultimate aim which he pursued was to
make himself emperor.

Preparations for the coronation had been made;

the crown which he was to wear lay at hand. Suddenly the provinces spoke up and threatened with declarations of independence; the empire came near going to pieces. Yuan Shikai died. They say he died a natural death.

Once a state of affairs has been reached where the voice of the people can be smothered by "silk frocks"; and where the power of the "strong man" rules—the mailed fist—should it not be possible, at such a time, for an old trooper to raise the imperial child to the throne? Old General Chang Chun was a trooper; and he had an army ready in his province. He was devoted to the old imperial house; a story was told that the Empress-Regent Tzu Hsi herself had discovered him, hearing some of his telling repartees, and had promoted him, from a horse groom, into an officer. Chang Chun suddenly proclaimed the restoration of the imperial child Hsuan Tung. The coronation took place. As he mounted the throne, the boy stumbled: an evil omen. Oh, well, a republic is better after all. Everyone has a passport to the highest office in the empire, provided he can at the right moment bare a mailed fist; and provided, as is the case, that the voice of the people is smothered under silken frocks. At the right moment, the president of the cabinet, Tuan

Shijui had the mailed fist. He deposed the new emperor and made himself Procurator of the Republic. Tuan Shijui also was a friend of the foreign powers. To please them, he declared war against Germany and went on deporting the Germans from China even after the armistice. What does one not do in order to please the "power of the purse in the land"? The national convention had become the playfield of the followers of more or less strong men, all of them aspiring to the presidency. There was an "Anfu party," a "Chili party," a party of the ministry of communications. Thus the empire was divided up, among the central organisations of the republic, into the domains of these party leaders. At last their armies fought for the possession of Peking and of the presidency; the national convention ceased to be the arena, which henceforth moved to the battlefield. China had a republic; but it had no longer a government.

Confucius says, "Without the confidence of the people in its rulers there can be no government of any kind." The present rulers did not even ask the people for its confidence; the voice of the people had been smothered.

II. THE BEQUEST OF SUN YATSEN

THEY say that faith can move mountains.

Supported by no other power but faith, Sun Yatsen now returned from Japan to Canton. There the faithful of the Kuo-Mintang gathered about him. They proclaimed an independent southern republic and declared a punitive war against the rulers of the north. A few military leaders, faithful to their ideals, joined them with their troops from the provinces of Kwang-Tung, Hu-Nan, and Yun-Nan. Sun Yatsen led them as president and commander-in-chief. Wu Tingfang was his chancellor and minister for exterior affairs.

Of the latter there were aplenty. The foreign powers looked disgruntled; the English neighbour at Hong Kong did what he could in order to stoke this wasps' nest with a long arm. The foreign consuls received orders from their governments not to deal with Wu Tingfang. The republic of southern China was not recognised. The foreigners relied upon the military governor of Canton, Chen Chiuming, and on the representatives of the Chinese merchant guilds and the chamber of commerce. The merchants of Canton were tied to Hong Kong by considerable trade interests. Chen Chiuming was riding the fence. He was afraid of the revolutionary spirit among the people of Canton and showed the Kuo-Mintang a friendly face. But at heart he was a militarist. He wished to be a factor in the game of the rulers of the North; and he conspired with them. He was the sort of man whom the English neighbour in Canton could make use of.

In the camp of the Kuo-Mintang a deep change of conviction had taken place. Experience had taught lessons. Nobody counted any longer on financial help from the foreign powers for the betterment of the economic conditions in China. Sun Yatsen attacked the task alone. First of all he wished to modernise the city of Canton. Wide streets were broken through the labyrinth of Chinese slums; the city "of the nights of terror" assumed the aspect of a European city, with parks and villas in the European style. Soon the foreigners moved from the English settlement on the island of Shameen into the new quarters of the city.

Even many offices were soon transferred into the six-storied concrete buildings which began to grow up on the banks of the Pearl River. Industries were to be founded. Next, Canton was to have a new harbour for deep-sea vessels; the river was to be dredged. It was planned to complete the railway from Canton to Hankau. For all this Sun Yatsen still figured to obtain at least foreign private capital. He granted industrial concessions on liberal terms; for he understood well that foreign capital wished to earn large and quick returns when it came to China; but on one condition he insisted implacably: that the Chinese government could at any time, by paying the price of purchase, re-acquire the foreign establishments. Nothing much has come of these concessions. Foreign capital was afraid of the political uncertainty.

Still more distinctly was the change of conviction in the camp of the Kuo-Mintang shown in its political relations to the foreign powers. Wu Tingfang was not the man to allow himself to be overlooked politically. He attacked every encroachment of the foreigners sharply; and there were plenty of them, on the part of the English neighbour at Hong Kong, as well as on the part of private merchants. Sun Yatsen stamped the slogan, "Down with Imperialism!" It meant not only an aggressive defence against the imperialistic rule of the foreigners in China but also the warlike conquest of all those forces native to the country itself which resisted the victory of the popular will. That slogan found an echo throughout the people.

But experience had taught Sun Yatsen other things which he now converted into action. The revolution had to strike deeper root. Within the middle class, the spirit of wealth, the desire to make money and to enjoy it in security had proved a barrier at which revolutionary convictions stopped short. The Chinese middle class was not reactionary in a stupid sense; nor was it incapable of enthusiasm. But as soon as the straight road of the least resistance in making money had to bend before the onslaught of what was politically new, that middle class turned unhesitatingly and decisively against everything which disturbed it in its material aspirations. That class saw in the administration of the empire first of all a means to give the material aspirations "of the people"—as they expressed it—an undisturbed security. Under the old régime that class had held power, as far as it went, and it enjoyed a freedom to get rich which was fortified by ancient custom. The desire to preserve

this state of affairs made it conservative without making it a conscientious and loyal follower of the
monarchy or hostile to the revolution. Briefly, the
middle class pursued its "business."

Sun Yatsen saw that he could not lean on the power
of this middle class. He recognised it as a class indispensable within the empire; as the class within which
intelligence and education found their soil. But it
had to be stripped of its power as a class. Whoever
saw no more in the form of the constitution than did
this middle class—he to whom it did not flow with
necessity from the national consciousness, as an expression of the spirit of the people—must willy-nilly
become an enemy to all happy government; he must
ultimately be sacrificed to the higher aspirations. The
domestic policy of the Kuo-Mintang now took for its
aim the strengthening of the labour guilds, their conversion into labour unions, and the institution of peasant associations. When news of the revolution of
Lenin in Russia reached Canton, Sun Yatsen saw at
once the far-reaching importance of events in that
quarter. He sent a telegram to a man whom he had
known in the days of his exile in Canada and who, in
turn, had known Lenin in his days of exile. Thus an
exchange of ideas came about between Sun Yatsen

83

and Lenin. Lenin induced the first ambassador of Soviet Russia to Japan, Joffe, to drop in on Sun Yatsen, in the spring of 1923. It was in consequence of this visit that, in the summer of 1923, a Soviet envoy by name of Borodin was sent to the republic of southern China at Canton.

At Canton this was a time of great faith and great distress. If there were no faith! Without faith there could be no storm and stress led by an idea to fight against everything that seems built for eternity. Great faith in the idea creates such fighters who can rarely win for themselves anything great but death. Anxiety for the daily bread gives them a patient and hopeful people. The rich middle class sought safety, with kith and kin, at Hong Kong. The little fellow had to remain behind. He had to look on when this new progress tore open half of his house in order to make room for new streets. He could do nothing but make his bargain with the future which would bring him an indemnity in the form of an unearned increment. So far the government had nothing to offer except the paper money of Chen Chiuming which was hardly worth anything. The coffers of the government were empty. The foreign powers held the only current sources of income, sea duties and salt duties,

GENERAL TANG SHENGCHIH

Sub-commander under Chiang Kaishek; leader of the expeditionary force against Wu-Chang and Hankau; defender of the nationalist capital Hankau; victor over the united armies of Chang Tzolin and Wu Peifu on the borders of Ho-Nan.

WU-CHANG ON THE YANG-TZE-KIANG

After the siege by the Nationalist Army

under lock and key; their men-of-war were anchored in the harbour of Canton, standing guard. Strikes directed against the English carrying trade and labour demonstrations followed each other. Deep disquietude took hold of the suspicious peasant who yet came to town and listened open-mouthed to the speeches that were being made. The peasant took much valuable lore back to the village.

But it was also a time of the greatest distress in Canton. The army clamoured for rice. The generals extorted levies of war from a patient and impotent people. All quarters of the city were invaded by gambling and opium. It is true that these things furnished duties for rice and munitions for the army; but from day to day the position became less tenable. Sun Yatsen gave the order which sent the army into the provinces. The punitive war against the north had begun, enforced by distress.

There they went forth, these mercenaries of the republic of southern China, in indigo-blue or grey jackets of cotton, the trousers rolled up to the knees, with munition belts on chest or back, rifle on shoulder. The sun burns down. The roads are narrow and clayey. Three feet wide, paved with uneven stone, thus the highways wind along between muddy fields of rice and over bare mountains which in the distance loom like a blue haze. No camp awaits the Chinese soldiers. In the dew of the night or in the drizzling rain they wait for the greying of dawn in the open field; or crowded together, shivering and crouching under the roof of a miserable mud-hut in some village. These villages are poor. The daily food comes directly from the field; there are no stores of anything. The soldier must carry what he needs, the kettle to boil water in, a little wood, a little basket full of rice or millet, not to forget the huge rain-hat. Hasn't the soldier enough to carry, what with the munitions which press on chest or back, what with the rifle on his shoulder? Let the peasants help! Like sheep from the pasture they are rounded up. In the loop of a long rope pulled by soldiers, they are caught in gangs and loaded with the baggage. On they go; rain drips from the rims of the huge bamboo hats, three feet in diameter, from the umbrellas of waxed paper, which wind like a snake without end through the landscape. Soldiers and carriers are barefooted; sandals of straw, soaked and discarded, strew the margin of the road. The march takes weeks. At last the soldier goes into battle. A city calls, not deserted as the villages had begun to be when he entered. Rumour travels fast in

China. News of the approach of a troop flies ahead; the peasants pack up and flee with whatever can be carried away. In the city there are billets with fresh rice, and plunder. In a scattered formation the troops approach the walls that surround the city, firing. Machine guns clatter: the garrison of some general who follows one of the northern rulers gets ready for defence. Dead and wounded fall. There they lie or crawl on. Such is the soldier's lot.

In this campaign the walls of many a city had to be stormed with ladders, against the fire of the machine guns; for the army needed rice; it needed the munitions and the arms of the garrison. Every soldier knew that; and he knew also that the city population would pay him his arrears in order to escape the sack. Thus the army of the Kuo-Mintang conquered the two provinces of Kwang-Tung and Kwang-Si for the republic of southern China and advanced to the border line of the province of Kiang-Si.

In the field, the commander-in-chief received the disastrous news of the apostasy of the governor and military commander of Canton, Chen Chiuming. It is hard to say in detail whether the capitalists that had fled from Canton seduced Chen Chiuming; or whether Chen Chiuming took the first step and promised the wealth to suppress by force of arms the new aspirations after power of labour and peasantry, on condition that the wealth return from Hong Kong. Even how much help either of the two expected from the English neighbour, only those know who are wise enough to keep silent. It is certain that the three of them were united against the republic by the common desire to return to the old division of their power over conditions in Canton. All three relied upon it that the suffering poorer middle class would welcome them, parading as the friendly voice of the people. The political convictions of the suffering poorer middle class still fell into those scales where lay its own nearest interest.

Sun Yatsen left the army and hastened to Canton. Too late; his appeal to conscience bore no fruit. Chen Chiuming had declared himself. During the night of the 16th day of the sixth moon he had had the temple on the mountain slope where Sun Yatsen lived surrounded. Sun Yatsen knew of the intention; but a revolutionary idea does not yield before empty threats. Soon there was the sound of firing; the house burst into flames. Sun Yatsen was forced to flee. The city at his feet was in revolt. The soldiery of Chen Chiuming raided labor quarters and Kuo-Mintang. Sun Yatsen made a safe escape and reached a loyal gunboat on the river. He had taken leave of his wife; they had said good-bye forever. A young drummer and a soldier of the small bodyguard of Sun Yatsen fired, from the window of the house of the women, on the invading people of Chen Chiuming. Through dark and narrow streets they led Sun Yatsen's wife into the city. The soldier fell dead at her side, hit by a bullet. In the hut of a peasant the brave woman found a disguise; masquerading as a coolie woman she rejoined her husband. The news of her capture had preceded her. But Chen Chiuming's men had been mistaken in the person; and so the pursuit had been given up.

The following night brought a new danger. A mine which had floated down the river was discovered as by a miracle, from the ship on which Sun Yatsen was, a few seconds before it touched; it was pushed away. That small group of men which still represented the republic of southern China could no longer remain in Canton. Sun Yatsen went to Shanghai and waited there till reliable troops should have retaken Canton.

Soon the picture is changed again. Chen Chiuming risked no decisive battle with the leaders of the Kuo-Mintang who were returning; he withdrew a few miles

from the city, to the arsenal on the north river. Even
that was a strategic position threatening danger for
Canton. But Sun Yatsen returned to the city and
made his headquarters in the old cement factory, on
the far bank of the Pearl River which flows through
the city.

Must not he be called a great man who narrows
down for his people the limits of what its conscience
permits in public life? That was what Sun Yatsen
did by his example. At a time when Chen Chiuming
still stood within the power of the Kuo-Mintang, the
danger which might come from him for the cause had
been well known. Sun Yatsen had been hard-pressed
by those who surrounded him to "remove" that danger. Up to the very last years of the monarchy the
history of China had recognised political murder as
legitimate. Even in Canton there was poison. Sun
Yatsen forbade to talk of it. He was too great a man
to snatch at such means in order to save *himself;* the
cause *of the people* did not need them. Throughout
his whole political life the hands and the cause of Sun
Yatsen remained unpolluted by infamy; and for the
nationalistic government of the Kuo-Mintang this
rule has become a tradition.

Even now Sun Yatsen declined to oust Chen Chiuming from the arsenal by force of arms. So long as the just cause could *command,* he did not sacrifice a human life. He summoned Chen Chiuming to his headquarters. At last the man replied in a dutiful letter that he would come. And with the grey of dawn Chen Chiuming did appear before the gates of Canton, but with the whole of his army. The surprise was complete. The general of the garrison himself had to take rifle in hand; every bullet counted in this struggle for the possession of the city. Chen Chiuming was repulsed; his troops were scattered; he himself fled to Hong Kong.

But this was not the last which the republic was to suffer from Chen Chiuming. That wealth which had fled to safety furnished new means; the rulers of the north sent rifles and munitions; the English neighbour permitted an army to cross the territory of Hong Kong. Thus Chen Chiuming gathered new regiments on the west river, in the province of Kwang-Tung. Through the seaport of Swatow he pushed new troops, gathered in Shan-Tung and elsewhere, as far as the east river; and he occupied the city of Hwei-Cheu, about seventy-five miles from Canton. On all inland waterways came now the enemies of the republic; for an expeditionary force of Wu Peifu followed even the north river in its advance upon Canton.

The battle broke not far from Canton, on the railway leading north. The task confronting the mercenaries of Sun Yatsen, men from Yun-Nan and Hu-Nan, was overwhelming. They opposed, with munitions of a hundred cartridges per man, a superior enemy equipped with field guns, model troops from the days of Yuan Shikai. With fixed bayonets they advanced. Nobody fired. They were led by the firm determination to hold on to that little piece of land where they stood; as their homeland, Yun-Nan and Hu-Nan had long since fallen into the hands of the rulers of the North. Fifteen hundred feet from the enemy, the first shot was fired. Field guns, machine guns, and munitions were taken wholesale. The invader was thrown back into the rough mountains of Hu-Nan, beyond the end of steel. For the first time the peasant put hand to the wheel of his destiny in these fights. Armed with picks and ancient halberds, the peasants drove scattered troops of the enemy together, disarmed them, and handed them over to Sun Yatsen. Much precious lore had come from Canton into the village; open-mouthed the peasant had learned something; he had understood that his own cause was at stake. He furnished his contingent. Sun Yatsen called the peasants, not without pride, his "volunteers."

Along the west river Chen Chiuming's forces had meanwhile been driven into the province of Kwang-Si. Hwei-cheu, on the east river, was being besieged. It was a small city, surrounded by mediæval walls, situated in a broad morass. It was the birth-place of Chen Chiuming. The siege lasted two years. The technical resources of the republic and its free-lance warfare were insufficient to take the town or to cut it off from all communication with Chen Chiuming's base at Swatow. To bombard the town itself Sun Yatsen forbade. The people who lived there were innocent; they were the people of Sun Yatsen; they must not be injured.

Meanwhile the population of Canton suffered greatly from the feeling of insecurity. Wild rumours of the immediate nearness of the enemy would not permit the disquietude to go to sleep; the newspapers of Hong Kong kept expectation alive by daily reports of violent things which Chen Chiuming would shortly undertake. Every troop of soldiers on the march roused a new suspicion of near danger for the city. Chinese merchants as well as the foreigners had, at the time, nothing good to say of Sun Yatsen's régime. Business flagged. Confiscations of boats for troop transports and a spreading spirit of piracy among soldiers scattered along all lanes of traffic impeded the movement of goods and injured sensibly both import and export trade of the merchants. Even processions in the streets with which labour obtruded again made it a foregone conclusion that the accustomed business was to be still further obstructed. But whoever visited headquarters had these erroneous impressions at once wiped out: there, conscious hopefulness was the rule. Sun Yatsen's quiet conduct, placid even in danger, created about him an atmosphere of unquestioning confidence. Revolutionary aspirations, the work of destroying an old order to which all were devoted, here, with a serious will, assumed the face of a great task, of a duty not to be evaded. That savour of the reprehensible which clothes, for the law-abiding citizen, everything that is revolutionary, dropped like a disguising cloak which had been hung around a just cause. Here nobody made revolution for the sake of revolution. The most conservative proposals, made in order to help the people to procure a free seaport of its own, or the city corporation to

94

obtain an independent telephone line or wireless station, were joyfully welcomed. Every conversation with Sun Yatsen communicated this definite impression; he wanted nothing else but to create those conditions which were necessary for a higher existence of his whole people. He was a revolutionary only, because for that purpose he *had* to be one. This trait was not a mere sign of loyalty to his convictions; much less the inspiration of utilitarianism; it bore witness to a peculiarity of character in Sun Yatsen. That could be seen in many trifles. Thus it is the custom in China, when you visit a high official, to take a present along. Nobody ever thought of bringing Sun Yatsen anything of value. A little basket of particularly nice fruit; a new industrial product of the proletariat; or Chinese cigarettes which his wife might take down to the wounded soldiers;—such things were apt to win Sun Yatsen's friendliness. But even in world-politics, his character, sure of its aim, lifted him again and again above all formalities, so that the diplomats marvelled. Even in 1923 the following thing took place.

Sun Yatsen had made an attempt to take over the levying of the sea duties. At once English, French, and American marines had been landed from the war-

ships in the harbour and had prevented the confiscation of this resource pledged to the foreign powers. At headquarters in Canton, a conversation was
brought about with the American minister to China.
Sun Yatsen put up the question: what position China
was in, that the foreign powers levied dollars and cents
from the Chinese people and handed what was left
over, after they had deducted their own claims, to the
militarists at Peking to make war upon the people
who had paid these very levies? China had, he argued,
in these foreign powers, so many masters that no single one felt any responsibility. These remained deaf to
every protest. Indeed Korea had a master, Japan.
But at least this one master could not escape
those duties which the universal opinion of man imposes upon a "master" towards a "subject people."
The Chinese people owed no other debt to the foreign
powers but this one, that they had been overpowered
when the foreigners came in order to open the country
for their "democracy." Now the foreigners themselves prevented the people from ruling themselves
in China. If the foreign powers would come, to a man,
in order to institute a popular government and to introduce industries; if they would undertake, faithfully and truthfully, to withdraw of their own volition

whenever the Chinese people had learned to maintain an honest popular government, *then, said Sun Yatsen, he would place himself and all his followers into the service of such a cause and win over the nation to this plan.*

Even this passionate outburst remained without fruit. It even is like this whenever an armed dictate has been placed over a people, the armed power soon loses the consciousness of an obligation, such as the co-ordination of the nations imposes in the interest of peaceful life. The significance of a public opinion which, in the life of men, demands an indispensable consideration pales for him who holds the armed power. Then indeed do words of peaceful good-will sound without an echo. Sun Yatsen's offer of peace to the powers was killed by silence. Contemptuously they called him an idealist.

When, further, the dictate of power rests unbendingly upon the inner development of the life of a people; when its nearest road, the road of arms, remains permanently blocked, defence will finally have to turn against the soil itself in which the restricting power finds its anchorage. It will have to turn against the existing order in the country itself; and that is revolution. The step is no great one. The pressure of a foreign power upon the inner organs of a state prevents their growth for the benefit of the people. Confiscation of the revenue of state enforces levies which are out of proportion; soon the people as such, the man in the street, looks upon his own state as upon a ruthless expropriator of the fruit of labour. Even on the class of the well-to-do a shadow falls. In a world which is built on capital, it is the task of this class to finance the powers of labour of those who own nothing. But even capital carries its corresponding load; and since capital is its own neighbour, it will deny labour the prospect of bettering its living conditions. Thus a universal state of things arises which is tense enough for revolution. It was not otherwise in China. In the control and the dictate of the foreigners over such important sources of revenue as the customs duties, the revolution of 1911 had changed nothing. The amount of the sea duties (i.e. of the import and export duties) still remained in China at the old level which had been dictated by the foreigners; their levy remained in their hands. As compared with the provincial inland duties (the so-called river duties or Likin) which the Chinese merchant had to pay, the goods of the foreigners enjoyed considerable privileges; and the salt duty was subject to foreign confiscation. These duties amounted to almost half of the total revenue of China. Wherever the new government turned in order to open up new sources of revenue, there it met with the reservations of the international financial power. Only the well-to-do middle class had been helped by the revolution of 1911. But that middle class, whipped on by selfishness, tortured by jealousy, had divided into bitterly hostile camps and entrenched itself behind military leaders who fought for control of the empire. Thus the imperialistic rule had penetrated even the interior. The peasant, the workman, the disinterested lower middle class began to look upon their own state as upon a country visited by the tiger.

There was an enormous labour and peasant class which owned nothing. Easily seventy per cent of the peasants of China are tenants. Millions heard the call of Sun Yatsen to rise in revolution against the imperialism of the militarists, with their followers among the well-to-do, and against the imperialism of the foreign powers in China; the slogan of the revolution resounded, calling for the right to have part in the determination of the living conditions for all classes of the people within the empire.

Yet, Sun Yatsen had no communistic aims.

Of that doubts have often been voiced. But it is convincingly proved by that doctrine of his which he deposited in writing on the twelfth day of the fourth month of the thirteenth year of the republic. It says literally:

"My revolutionary doctrine of a popular government is rooted in three fundamental maxims and consists of the 'five offices of the people.'

"The first maxim treats of livelihood. The four necessities of life are food, clothing, shelter, and freedom of movement. These are to be the object of a common endeavour of people and government to feed the people by the development of agriculture and trade; to clothe it by the development of industries; to give it shelter by the development of the crafts; and to procure freedom of movement by the development of roads.

"The second maxim treats of the power of the people to rule. The government must educate the people to the point where it can rightly fill its office of appointing and of recalling officials and of deciding on and of vetoing measures.

"The third maxim treats of (Nationalism) the tasks of government. The task, for the government of the interior, consists in protecting the weak and in

100

taking measures for their self-preservation; for the government of the exterior, in warding off encroachments on the part of foreign nations, in abolishing unjust treaties, and in restoring the suzerainty of the empire and its equality with other nations.

"Government must go through three phases: (1) the military phase, (2) the educational phase, (3) the constitutional phase.

"During the military phase the existing resistance against good government must be swept away by force; and amongst the people must be propagated nationalistic unity.

"As soon as nationalistic unity has been achieved provincially the second phase must be entered. In this second phase, the government is to send officials who have been tested as to their abilities into all districts of the province to help the people to organise self-government. For this it is necessary to count the population, to survey the land, to build roads, and to organise a police force. A people of a district which, firstly, knows how to make use of its rights and whose civic education, therefore, has been finished; which, secondly, has accepted the revolutionary doctrine; which, thirdly, knows how to elect municipal officers, for the purpose of self-administration, and, fourthly,

101

knows how to elect delegates for a legislative council of the community—such a people has achieved self-government.

"In such a self-governing district, the citizens shall fulfil their task of electing and dismissing officials, and of enforcing or repealing their own decrees.

"The people in self-governing districts are to undertake the assessment of real property and its taxation. At that local government must have the power to acquire real property at assessed values wherever the value of land rises by reason of public expenditure; or it has the right to raise taxation in order to utilise the unearned increment for the public weal and not to let it remain for the profit of the private owner only.

"Revenues growing out of taxes on real estate; unearned increment of the latter, income derived from public lands, public forests, waterways, water-powers, and mines are the property of the government and are to be used to develop commerce, old-age insurance, insurance against disability, and the care for orphans and those in distress.

"The utilisation of mining resources in the country and the establishment of great industrial and commercial enterprises for which district means are insufficient are to be financed by the central government, on the principle of a division of profits.

"The amounts of the subsidies to be paid by the districts to the central government are to be fixed by the delegates of the districts; they are to be not less than ten and not more than fifty per cent of the total revenues of the district.

"Every self-governing district is to send a delegate to the central government.

"All officials of a district must have passed an examination conducted by the central government.

"As soon as self-governing districts have been erected, we reach the third phase of a nationalist government in which the people elect provincial presidents of the government board to act as the highest supervisors of the provincial government. In all questions which concern the whole empire, these presidents are to be subordinated to the central government.

"The differentiation between provincial and central government is to consist in this, that the former decides in provincial affairs, the latter in affairs concerning the whole empire.

"The district is the unit of self-government of the

country and the provincial government is to form the connecting link between the government of the districts and the central government.

"The central government is to be divided into five departments (Yuan) to enact the 'five offices' of the people, as follows: administration, legislation, jurisdiction, examination, control.

"The administration is to be subdivided into ministries as follows: (1) of interior affairs; (2) of exterior affairs; (3) of the army; (4) of finance; (5) of mines and agriculture; (6) of industry and commerce; (7) of public worship; (8) of traffic.

"Before a constitution can be put into force, these offices must loyally and firmly adhere to the president (Sun Yatsen).

"The legislative is to work out a constitution founded upon the revolutionary doctrine and upon the achievements of the first two phases of government. The draft of the constitution is to be communicated to the people in such sections as arise from time to time.

"When more than half of all the provinces of the empire have entered upon the third phase, provincial government can be considered as (practically) established; and a national convention can be called together from among the district delegates in order to adopt and to proclaim the constitution.

"As soon as the constitution has been proclaimed, the right of appointment to the central government is transferred from the president (Sun Yatsen) to the national convention.

"With the proclamation of the constitution the third phase of government is completed. Then the people must proceed to the constitutional election (of the head of the state and of the ministers one for each of the five functions). Three months after the election the national convention dissolves itself; and henceforth the constitutional government wields the power of the state."

· · · · · · ·

Perhaps we may contemptuously dispose of this programme as being "nothing new." To the Chinese, the proclamation of a popular government is none the less revolutionary, none the less the mighty deed of a great man. After Sun Yatsen's death this "thesis of the three revolutionary maxims" took on the significance of a political bequest. It must not be forgotten that in China there has been for centuries an absolutist bureaucracy which could forbid the people, on pain of death, to discuss politics in the tea houses. To the great mass of the common people, the ideas of Sun Yatsen seemed terrifyingly bold. It looked up to him as to a saint sent by heaven in order to do away with the bitterness of its lot on earth; it believed in his doctrine and absorbed it thirstily. Such an expectant humanity revealed itself that it raised Sun Yatsen again and again, out of moments of discouragement, to a life-long devotion and self-sacrifice. He has often said so. "I am myself the son of a poor man; whoever knows, like myself, what the peasants suffer, cannot help being a revolutionary." Without a revolutionary subversion which divested the well-to-do of their traditional task to finance the labour of those who had nothing, and which, therefore, usurped their importance for the government, the working population could not hope for any improvement in the conditions of its collective life. Sun Yatsen knew that not even western industry—being a capitalistic institution—could bring any change. The mentality of the well-to-do can never let go of the idea of a ruler, bred as it is by their own superior material condition. Interference by force is needed in order to convert it back to the God-given recognition of the fact that the social significance of capital for man is that of an obligation, not of a right over others. The ideas of Marx had imposed themselves upon Sun Yatsen, when he was abroad, not without convincing him; but his methods of fight, class warfare and the dictatorship of the proletariat, he refused to accept. His China lived, as far as conscious and deliberate class policies went, in a state of innocence. If the Chinese people could be delivered from that imperialism which had as it were grown wild in nature, then it could, by a superior education, be led around this abyss. That is the deep meaning of the bequest of Sun Yatsen. The appeal to humanitarianism inherent in it gives him a mind-moving power which sweeps the Chinese off their feet. Sun Yatsen fought for industries controlled by the state. He aimed at a state-capitalism; but without doing away with private property, without removing private initiative of all classes from the life of the people.

Sun Yatsen towered above the bewildering turmoil of active forces which were at work in Canton—with his mature insight, with his firm determination in all his actions and against all impediments, he towered in an often lonely greatness, "the resting pole within the flight of appearances." Day and night the actors in

the revolutionary movement came and went at headquarters. Military leaders appeared in the blinding
light or the obscuring shadow of the fortunes of war.
Political news items fluttered down to the table; move
after move, here stealthily, there in open attack, proceeded this game on which was staked what was to be
or not to be. Intercalated between such things there
took place consultations with the delegations of labour
unions, or with merchants and industrials, with the
aim of unfolding the creative forces of the people.
Financial care formed the never-changing background of the scene.

This sort of life at headquarters demanded much of
even healthy nerves; Sun Yatsen suffered. But nobody has ever seen him nervous. At a place least to
be expected lurked danger for his life. Two adven-
turous Americans had erected an air-craft shop for
Sun Yatsen. At a review of the planes, fire broke out
in an unexplained fashion; and Sun Yatsen had
hardly set foot into the open when the whole building
collapsed, with a sheaf of flame shooting high up into
the air. Sun Yatsen's first question was whether anyone had been killed. "The shop must be rebuilt at
once," he said next and went on. Perhaps he regarded
his life as charmed till his task would be completed;

he never thought of his suffering. His associates and the people believed that the master stood under the protection of his destiny; his escapes from almost certain danger to life had been next to miraculous.

Once, while boating on the Pearl River, Sun Yatsen's launch overtook a string of munitions-transports. The fortifications of Hwei-cheu were to be bombarded. Sun Yatsen was just speaking of the loyalty and reliability of the young flyer who was leading the expedition, when a sudden tremour ran through the launch and a moment later was wildly tossed about on the waves. The munitions had exploded and disappeared without leaving a trace. How Sun Yatsen's launch escaped destruction has not yet been explained.

Next day the body of the young aviator was found in the airport, washed ashore below his plane. "Even in death he wished to show me his loyalty," said Sun Yatsen with mystic conviction.

This august placidity was greatly enhanced by the fearlessness with which Sun Yatsen's wife stood by him in this troublesome life. She was a delicate, distinguished figure. Few words, but a winsome smile gliding eloquently through her pale, spiritual face bade the friendly caller welcome; behind her simplicity a true Chinese nobility was hidden, added to the best European breeding. In that she became a model for modern Chinese women. That strait-laced formality which assigned to the Chinese women, even then, the part of a mute statue whenever others but those belonging to the family were present, created an appearance as little adapted for public life as the bobbed femininity, devoid of all feeling for form, which returned from abroad, from schools and universities, to China. Sun Yatsen's wife wished to see transplanted into the Chinese family the spirit of a freer order, thence to be reflected into public life as culture. She wanted to change woman's allotted life; not the virtue of woman as established in ancient China. By lectures and speeches delivered in schools and assemblies of women she spread her mission; and she called upon the girls and women of China to raise their voices, too, in order to remodel conditions of life. There is, today, no political demonstration in China in which women and girls do not take their part.

The example set by Sun Yatsen's wife was no less revolutionary for the Chinese than the work of her husband. She had married from her own choice; she had followed her wedded husband into exile. Now she stood, visible to everybody, by his side in public: a thing unheard-of; for in old China the sexes were strictly separated. Women belonged in the inner chambers of the house; outside of the narrowest family circle, they were excluded from contact with men, from social intercourse, from the banquet of guests. Marriage was decided by the parents; in a closed and densely veiled palanquin the bride was carried into the house of the mother-in-law; and there she saw her husband for the first time. A separate household for newly-married people did not exist. By her marriage contract—by sharing a beaker of wine with the groom —the bride became the servant of her mother-in-law; she had to remain within the house of her parents-in-law even though her husband be called abroad by his work. It is nothing rare in China for married couples to be separated for years.

But one thing was non-existent in ancient China that the new social order will have to cope with. There has never been a sex problem. There was no room for it. But whoever draws the conclusion from that that in China there were more unhappy marriages than elsewhere is mistaken. Nature had its rights.

Custom united the sexes in marriage at the age of

111

sixteen or eighteen; within the protection of the parent home, and in a total exclusion of the women from intercourse, they were allowed to find their way side by side into family life; and nearly always there arose a youthfully warm friendship and mutual affection lasting for life. With the birth of a son the young woman assumed an importance of her own for the family. She was no longer a servant; she was the mother who propagated the race; hers were the honours and joys of motherhood, hers the happiness of a wife.

It is true that the co-habitation of many families, within the necessarily limited space of the family home, often proved not easy. We Europeans, with our need for independence, should soon find it unbearable. But the Chinese, in their millennia-old culture, have a remedy.

There was a family of six thousand souls, offspring of nine brothers, whose happy life-in-common was rumoured far and wide. Their fame reached the emperor. He resolved to see for himself; and he found, in the poverty of a Chinese village, nothing but peaceful and joyous men. He asked the oldest how this was possible. Calling for paper and brush, this man wrote Chinese letters all over the sheet. The emperor read. He found one word written a hundred times, "Tolerance." "From the first awakening of the understanding," thus declared the old man, "we teach our children tolerance and consideration for the peculiarities of brothers and sisters." That is no more than Confucian doctrine applied to action. The master taught, "See to it that the character be confirmed in the ways of right living. Without care of the due forms of intercourse reverence becomes theatrical, reserve becomes timidity, boldness mutiny, sincerity coarseness."

The social structure of the old China was thus closely interwoven with religious ideas. But it was in this old China where Sun Yatsen worked. To react to his figure and his work even as approximately as his people reacted to them, we must first of all try to arrive at the point of view of the Chinese people. Then we shall understand many a phenomenon in the policies of Sun Yatsen and his successors which must for ever remain enigmatic while we judge from our European point of view.

Classicism—the religious and political foundation of the Chinese state—with which Sun Yatsen found himself face to face came from way back at the beginning of the second century before Christ, when the

113

last ruler of the Ts'in dynasty had drowned feudal-
ism, dominant till then, in torrents of blood and raised
himself to the throne in the year 221 B.C. On this, the
task to organise a new empire had fallen to the suc-
ceeding Han dynasty. A foundation was found in the
classical books which Confucius had either collected or
annotated during the fifth century before the birth of
Christ. Under the influence of the historical books,
there grew, out of the mystic-religious "Book of
Metamorphoses," out of the "Canon of the Odes,"
and out of the "Ritual of the forms of intercourse,"
the Confucian edifice of state, which had been inherited from dynasty to dynasty, and had lasted down
to the days of Sun Yatsen. In it, the religious theses
of the classical books had been raised into a state religion; they formed the religious and political foundation for the bureaucratic system of government China
had down to the Manchus.

The religious ideas themselves, contained in these
books, were still older. For in the classical book of history we read that King Shun offered the customary
sacrifices as early as 2255 B.C.; that he offered sacrifices to the ancestors, the mountains and rivers, and to
all spirits. Philosophical meditations about God—why
there is a God; where God's throne is; or why man

114

must obey God's commandments—are no longer contained in the classical books. The Chinese idea of a Shang-Ti or Lord of the Heavens, also called Tien or Heaven (that which is above man) is met with as given from immemorial, prehistoric times.

The king offered sacrifice to heaven, to almighty God; he offered it in the open, for God is everywhere. There were no other priests. The people erected temples for their ancestors, and there worshipped their own forefathers. Nature, on the other hand, was conceived as animated by spirits whose protection and aid could be won by all by sacrifices offered in the open. Thus the world of the Chinese was ruled by an impersonal, monistically conceived God of whom the spirits of nature were a part. Whatever happened to man, happened through God. Social fetters were imposed by God; moral law sprang from Him. Fate or providential dispensation was unknown among the Chinese; there was no word for it in the classical books.

This primitive religion—a community with God as the source of all men did and all that happened in the world—was preserved as late as the Chow dynasty, 1125 B.C. From then on God steps back and ultimately disappears from the religious consciousness of the Chinese; all that happens in the world is explained now by the philosophic-dualistic principle of Yang and Yin. With the proclamation of the identity in God of "Father Heaven" and "Mother Earth" it assumes its rule over the Chinese mind. Twofold is the breath of the universe. Yang is heavenly light, warmth, fruitfulness, and life. Yin is the earth, darkness, cold, and death. The birth of living beings is a blending of Yang and Yin. Men, animals, plants, mountains, water, and fire, every smallest particle is animated by the breath of the universe and *Tao,* the way by which the dualistic "one" manifests itself, the order of heaven, is the creator of all phenomena in the universe. It is the moving power in the circling of stars, in the change of the seasons, in life and death. Immutably just is Tao to all beings and men; it begets them and protects them and leads their souls back into the universe.

Then, during the fifth century before the birth of Christ, the road of the One forked in two directions in Chinese philosophy.

Lao-Tze taught the imitation of Tao. A true Taoist is he who binds within himself the forces of the universe through virtue. The breath of the universe penetrates all creation; the Athmos is in the

SUN FO

*Son of Sun Yatsen from a first marriage, mayor of Canton and
minister of commerce in the Nationalist Government*

RENOVATED CHINA

Before the gates of the Forbidden City of Peking

air, in plants and animals and stones; and the wise man gains, through a life near nature, through deep breathing, by the right use of plants and things the elixir of life; and he can enter the realm of the immortal. Taoism has placed high ideals of virtue and self-denial before the Chinese. But it has also seeded among the people the popular religion of a mystic fear of spirits who lurk in the air, in the tops of trees, in water, in the house, in all things, waiting for man in order to bring him ill fortune; it has created a priesthood which exorcises devils with magic formulæ, which heals diseases and conjures ghosts, thus keeping awake within the people the most variegated superstitions.

Confucius, on the other hand, would have none of supernatural things and spirits. When he had conversed with Lao-Tze, he said to one of his disciples, "I know that birds fly, that fish swim, and that animals run. Remains the dragon. How the dragon, through wind and cloud, rises into heaven, I do not know. I have today seen Lao-Tze; and I can only compare him to the dragon."

Confucius conceived heaven as "abstract justice." In the "Book of Metamorphoses" it is written, "The infinite created the beginning; the beginning created

117

the two principles; and these created the universe. Yang is movement; Yin is rest. Out of movement and rest, out of action and inaction in their interchange arises the universe. The revolution of change forms the matter of the universe; it calls the dead to life and the living to rest, or into other forms of being." That is the "road" of heaven. The "road" of man also lies in nature, in his physical and mental being; it is prescribed by heaven and immutable. Heaven has placed the five relations between men, viz., that between ruler and people, father and son, and those between brothers and sisters and among friends. Man's soul, created by the Tao, is good from the beginning. The essence of his being has flown from the four fundamental principles of heaven, and fourfold is the essence of human being. It exists in the sympathy of the heart at sight of a suffering neighbour and teaches mutual toleration; it exists in the feeling of shame and guilt, under the name of righteousness. As good-breeding it exists in the feeling of modesty and consideration; and as reason it exists in our judgment of good and evil. The essence of human being is the source of moral law. Men whose lives are ordered in harmony with the essence of morals live at one with heaven; they live happily in

118

the five mutual relations of men; for there is no happiness in this world except in the social virtues. In them reside reward and punishment as dealt out by heaven. King and officials existed by virtue of a mandate of heaven which had given them the task to enforce the laws of heaven among men.

As according to prehistoric tradition life did not cease with a complete dissolution of body and soul, the soul, born by a spontaneous confluence of Yang and Yin, returned into the universe; and for those left behind the presence of the dead need not cease. Thus it was a filial duty to sacrifice to the ancestors; it was a filial duty to beget male descendants, that the race might be preserved, and the sacrifices of the race. The mother of a son enjoyed special honour in the family. Such Confucius received the worship of the ancestors within his religious and political doctrine. At first sight that may look strange. It was done from the knowledge that there is, in the soul of the people, a mystic desire; and it had for its aim the guidance of the forces which are liberated in the life of the people by the supernatural into lines which would help to preserve the state. When the worship of ancestors was elevated into state religion, the observation of the virtues of the fourfold essence of human

119

life was confirmed by law and government, and as a heaven-given foundation of morals, ethics, and politics, within the five mutual relations of men, was made sacred as religious observance of the people.

Thus had Confucius derived, from the metaphysical essence of what happens in the world, an absolute authority of moral law, binding upon people and rulers; the cultivation of the personality and the general law of life coinciding in the canon of a great idea of culture from which then rose the Confucian state.

It is easily understood that neither Lao-Tze's Taoism nor a religion imposed from without and lacking these foundations of morals, ethics, and politics for a collective life could ever take hold of the whole soul of the Chinese. At times there was in China a considerable Jewry; today it is completely absorbed. The religion of Mohammed and the religion of Buddha were never able to captivate more than that side of the Chinese soul which inclined to mysticism; the materialistic translation of feeling and belief, that essence through which they rooted in reality, remained unshaken. There are also many Christians in China. Sun Yatsen himself was a Christian. The ethical principles of Christianity must necessarily win over Chinese character which is predestined for all that is moral. But Christ demanded that man free himself, for the sake of salvation, from the bonds of the world and the family. But the Chinese people did not care to see its reality perish in such a Christianity; nor had Christianity, in the form of the Christian-capitalistic powers, made its appearance in China as even bringing decided worldly happiness. The Confucian spirit, with its demand for the *right devotion* to that which is given in the world, erected too high an ideal for the character of man as such and for his citizenship within the state, for Sun Yatsen, the man or the statesman, to wish for its replacement, within the Chinese people, by a Christian doctrine.

People and rulers, in Confucianism, both stand under the absolute obligations of a religious-worldly system of morals. The ruler retains the heavenly mandate of government only while he uses it for the benefit of the people. The right of might has never been acknowledged, in this China of five thousand years, as being a justification, by fact or right, for any ruler. We read in the "Canon of Odes": "Does not the verdict of annihilation hang above those (autocrats) whom heaven knows not?" There are many examples in the Book of History. Chow Sin, ruler of China up to 1122 B.C., devastated the land by his excesses; the people sank into misery. T'a Ki, his mistress, was as beautiful as a lotus flower. But she was lewd and cruel. She seduced the king into unheard-of expenditure; so that the people groaned under taxes and levies. Whenever anyone murmured in protest, T'a Ki had him seized and driven over the "roaster." That was an invention of her own. It was a copper roller rotating over a huge grating of glowing charcoal. Ecstatically she watched the agony of her victims. Prince Wu of Chow revolted. Thus he addressed his assembled friends, "Heaven and earth are father and mother of the universe. Of all beings man is the highest. Among men he who has understanding and reason is chosen ruler. He is called to rule in order that he may be father and mother to the people. King Chow is devoid of all reverence for heaven and its laws; he tortures the people on earth. Heaven commands us to annihilate him; for heaven sees with the eyes of the people and hears with the ears of the people. Because I demur, the people murmur against me. The curse of heaven will do away with King Chow; and I call upon you to assist me in executing the command of heaven." In spring of 1123 Prince Wu marched eastward and stormed the capital. In the tower of the hunting lodge of T'a Ki, Chow Sin burned himself to death.

As upon the deed of Prince Wu, thus the Chinese people looked upon the work of Sun Yatsen. As soon as the people recognised that Sun Yatsen demanded nothing for himself, everything for the people, it began to see in him one who was sent by heaven in order to better conditions for the poor; it was willing to follow him. But to guide the people towards communistic aims was not within Sun Yatsen's plans. There was an enormous class of workmen and peasants in China who owned absolutely nothing; it could well have been led toward a dispossession of all other classes and toward a dictatorship of the proletariat. Sun Yatsen, however, did not aim at revolution for the sake of revolution. He could not see a betterment of the condition of the poor in a decapitalisation of the whole country; and that would have been the consequence of a dispossession of the well-to-do. The religious and political foundation of the state in old China offered the bolshevist principle of state a certain amount of help rather than any considerable resistance. For capital had not yet seized upon the constitution of the bureaucracy. The ruler appointed

123

all officials. Nor did, so far, the well-to-do have the precedence, in offices of state, over those who owned nothing. Ability was tested without respect of persons, in strict state examinations; even the study of the classical books was not so expensive a preparation for the examinations as to make it accessible only to the well-to-do. As a matter of fact, a considerable number of the officials came from the villages and from among the poor. But for this very reason the spirit of old China was not inclined towards class warfare. Sun Yatsen considered the dictatorship of a class as a road which could not be trodden. It was not the case that China had had a quarrel with that philosophy of life on which the old institutions of state were founded; or that all culture values which China possessed had to be eradicated in order to make room for an entirely new philosophy of life. That the old Chinese culture of soul and mind made happier men than the mechanistic views of the West, no Chinese doubted. What had happened was this: the geographical and political territory of China had, through the development of the means of transportation on the part of the West, been moved within the sphere of influence of the will and the power of these foreigners; and the Chinese, therefore, could no longer retain their old order without losing their independent existence. China was like a provincial who, transplanted into the aggressive turmoil of a great city, must either adapt his active life to that turmoil or be torn limb from limb. Sun Yatsen wished to unite the whole people, middle class, peasants, and workmen, within a democratic constitution, in order that it might, with a serried front, preserve its own culture and adopt from the West only as much as it could use without interfering with its peculiarities for the blessing and benefit of the common people and no more. The republican constitution adopted after the revolution of 1911 had failed in this respect.

It had become evident that China could, from the democratic form of the western state, not gain the hoped-for stiffening of its front against the outside world. The essence of democracy had proved fatal for China: that determination of the conditions of life, operating through parliamentary methods, and led by forces with a capitalistic orientation. For in the interior, where the counterpoise of a proletariat with an equivalent political organisation was missing, democracy had raised military power and the influence of capital into wilful autocracy.

But Sun Yatsen turned at last to bolshevist

methods. Through an organisation of the proletariat a foundation was deliberately to be created for the enforcement of a state doctrine of the three revolutionary maxims.

Among the associates of Sun Yatsen in Canton much had been changed by that time. Wu Tingfang had died full of years. Of the eminent leaders of the original revolutionary society Tung Meng Hui few were left. The task to penetrate the present and to point the way into the future rested well-nigh on Sun Yatsen alone. There was Wang Chingwai whom the revolution of 1911 had freed from prison. By his experiences with western democracy he had been pushed still farther away than Sun Yatsen from his original political position; he leaned now towards the communistic doctrines. Another who belonged to the same group was Hu Hamming, one-time civil governor of Canton. He was a faithful follower of Sun Yatsen; but he could not quite divest himself of the old autocratic way of the officials of the old régime. Besides, there had been added younger forces, consisting chiefly of such sons of the country as had been educated in America and England. The post of minister of foreign affairs for Sun Yatsen was now held by Dr. C. C. Wu, son of Wu Tingfang. America

had made him into a diehard lawyer. Among the foreigners in China was Eugene Chen (Chen Yuren),
confidant and political secretary of Sun Yatsen, most
widely known through his journalistic activity.
Raised in England, in a Jesuit school; he was a gen-
tleman of the very best education, a clever writer with
a politically brilliant training. Sun Fo, son of Sun
Yatsen from a first marriage, educated in America,
acted as mayor of the city of Canton. There was no
finance minister; but Soong Tzevung (T. V. Soong),
a young brother-in-law of Sun Yatsen, had come to
Canton in order to introduce a better method of collecting the salt duties which Sun Yatsen had managed to withdraw from the watchful control of the
foreigners. He was upright and straight-forward;
and, having soon won the confidence of the merchants,
he knew how to increase the revenues flowing from
the salt monopoly considerably. For this office, his
attendance at the University of Harvard and his later
work as a practical banker, both in America and
Shanghai, had given him a thorough training. Side
by side with the military leaders of the old school, a
young officer, Chiang Kaishek, attracted attention.
He held no command. At headquarters he appeared as
adviser; but when his proposals went unregarded, he

disappeared again. Yet every misadventure brought him back to Sun Yatsen's side. He was stubborn but loyal, a firm adherer to the revolutionary cause. He had been educated in Japan and could not be counted among the most modern; but unlike Hu Hamming, he yet appeared not disabled, by a bureaucratic disposition, from grasping the far-reaching intentions of Sun Yatsen. A strange character was Liao Changkai. Born in San Francisco, he was nevertheless a thorough-going Chinese. He was the outspoken leader of the labour unions and succeeded in attaching labour to Sun Yatsen and to induce the workmen to organise. He was a revolutionary leader of the first order.

The august seriousness with which Sun Yatsen served his mission had gathered about him a circle of serious and sterling men. Nothing like pseudo-education or Pigeon-English was to be found at headquarters. Such men were needed. For with the downfall of the god-like authority of the emperor, with the disintegration of the bureaucratic discipline from above, the intriguing character of the Chinese had come to the fore throughout the empire. Spontaneous subordination to a cause was a thing which had not been taught in old China. To the prospect of self-glorification, the common weal was sacrificed without hesitation. This inclination could be derived from the old régime. Everything in the world was the property of the Son of Heaven, the emperor. On every official, down to the elder of a village, fell some reflection of this conceit. But by the force of tradition which prescribed the strictest formalities, it had been held in check in administrative details; the necessity of a painstaking observation of form in the intercourse between officials of different rank enforced a rigid discipline in the limitation of the power of each individual. Such a system did not train character in the bureaucracy; and as soon as the formal restraints had fallen in the revolution of 1911, intriguing ambitions and high-handed autocracy became apparent. Such was not only the case among the great and little rulers who now fought openly against each other: it was also the reason why the Kuo-Mintang proved so weak when it came to enforce its principles beyond the narrow limits of Canton. There was no unified power of party, finance, or army. The Kuo-Mintang was a loose band of followers of Sun Yatsen. Similarly, the revolutionary army was a loose association of individual generals with a common interest; they maintained their troops personally and for that purpose levied money from the population of whatever district these troops occupied. Money at the disposal of Sun Yatsen proceeded exclusively from the salt duties, the mayoralty, and the revenues of the civil governor. Whatever power Sun Yatsen had over the military and within the Kuo-Mintang was no more than the power of a towering personality. He had long seen how necessary it was to disentangle these things. Since the achievements of Germany during the World War had greatly impressed him, he sent, in 1922, an officer, the later superintendent of the arsenal at Canton, to Germany. He wanted to try whether he could win over that organising talent which had there become free through the end of the World War. That intention failed by reason of the lack of money without which nothing could be done in Germany at the time and by reason of the attempt of Chen Chiuming against Canton. Abroad, confidence in the cause of Sun Yatsen had once more sunk down to zero. Later, in the fall of 1924, a few Germans, privately engaged, did go to Canton; but they found the field occupied by the Russian delegation; and they could no longer achieve leadership.

Borodin and the Russian delegation have done well by the cause of Sun Yatsen. They introduced methodical order. First of all, was the Kuo-Mintang consolidated into a real party. Lists were prepared; and members inscribed themselves for a nominal fee and for the duration of a year. That inscription was to be repeated annually, so that, by-and-by, the leaders of the party would gain control over the reception or exclusion of members of the party. Throughout the empire, wherever possible publicly, but secretly where hostile rulers held sway, local branches of the party were formed and party offices installed. These had the task to serve as collection agencies and centres of propaganda. At last there was a systematic propaganda of the doctrines of Sun Yatsen, a political agitation against the rulers of the empire, an organisation of peasants and workmen, of pupils and students into unions. Thus the Kuo-Mintang grew slowly, like the communistic party in Russia, into a club or order which spread throughout the empire a certain uniformity of ideas and of political action; and which could expect from its members an organised devotion to the cause and a loyal willingness to make sacrifices, sometimes to sacrifice even life. In January 1924 the first party convention of the reorganised Kuo-Mintang was held; on May 1st, the first convention of labour unions was opened.

Next in importance, steps were taken to organise

the army. With the assistance and on the advice of the Russian delegation, Sun Yatsen opened during the same year a cadet school near Canton, on the island of Whang-Poa in the Pearl River. Chiang Kaishek was appointed principal. Russian military teachers gave instruction; Russia loaned apparatus; and above all she introduced modern methods of education to Whang-Poa. There, officers were to be trained coming from the lower middle class of the country, officers who would no longer be a mere gang of leaders of mercenaries but men with a political and military education. Military training was combined with political education. Soon young men, youthfully fiery, arrived from all the party centres in the empire.

Even in the standing army there was political propaganda: and soon soldiers could be seen in the streets addressing the common people with political harangues. The street became the arena of politics. Demonstrations and processions for which, since time immemorial, the Chinese people have shown a particular predilection, displayed banners with political slogans and carried about the colours of the Kuo-Mintang: a red field with the rising sun of Sun Yatsen on a blue background; public meetings in which tens of thousands took part, stump speeches of male and female students and workmen gave a moving picture of the effect which the bolshevist method of educating the people had among the Chinese.

Even at headquarters the influence of the methodical spirit of the Russians became apparent. Sun Yatsen succeeded in bringing about a resolution by which individual military leaders renounced the right to levy contributions on the people. Thus a beginning was made in consolidating finances within Sun Yatsen's hand. Military operations, too, were to be worked out and guided, more than heretofore, by a military council. General Galen came from Russia with a number of officers of the Russian general staff. A spirit of readiness for battle entered the revolutionary government of Canton.

Meanwhile there had also been a certain consolidation among the mandarin rulers in the north of the empire. Chang Tzolin had, in the three outer provinces of Manchuria, north of the Chinese wall, risen to the position of a monarch. His headquarters were at Mukden, where he conducted a government along the lines of the provincial constitutions of old China. By reason of his absolute independence he could unimpededly seize the revenues of these three rich provinces; and thus he was financially the strongest one among those who were rivals in the fight for the rule of China. He used his means for the building-up of a strong army. He built arsenals, munitions factories, wireless stations and military hospitals. Army equipment he imported from Europe, from steel helmet to trench tools. The foreign powers, it is true, had placed an embargo on the importation of war materials into China; and through the maritime customs they exercised a strict control over all imports. But spirits subservient to Chang Tzolin —such as were to be found even at the customs offices of Niu-Chwang, the seaport of Manchuria, in the Gulf of Liao-Tung—knew how to remedy that. Neither did Chang Tzolin hesitate to unload ships bringing war materials somewhere along the coast, under military guard. Japan's sphere of interest runs right through Manchuria; and Japanese supervision was not too watchful; the foreign powers protested at no time very vigorously.

Mukden was an eldorado for adventurers from all parts of the world. There were Russian royalists who had fled from the bolshevists in Siberia. There were men and women of every type. Champagne flowed in streams. There was the English General Sutton who built trench mortars for Chang Tzolin—an invention of his own—and wasted a fortune in that Mukden which had become so frivolous in the ways of the world. German engineers, French flyers, Japanese officers—all the world helped to build and to raise the power of the King of Manchuria. Meanwhile it was being said that Chang Tzolin could neither read nor write. But that is not true. Indeed, in his youth he had been secretary to a leader of bandits, by name of Chang Tzolin, a Hung-Hu-Tze. The Chinese government had promised this bandit a position in the army if he would cease from his activities. Such things happened in China. The bandit did not trust these advances; in his place his secretary surrendered to the authorities; and thus he entered the Chinese army under the name of Chang Tzolin, to rise till he was the uncrowned king of Manchuria. What he lacked in statesmanship, he made up for by a robber's cunning; whatever would not bend had to break; and Chang Tzolin ruled as a "strong man" in his part of the chaotically disrupted state of China.

Peking—with the so-called central power of the empire, the imperial officers who alone were recognised by the foreign powers, and the ministerial cabinet—lived in the shadow of the rifles of the self-appointed president of the empire, Tsao Kun and his generals Wu Peifu and Feng Yuhsiang. In the face of the total disintegration of governmental power in China, the foreign powers still held on to the fiction of a central government. On the occasion of a question to the government in the British parliament—the question being *which* government of China British remonstrances had been addressed to—the English secretary of foreign affairs answered, "There is only one government in China." That the foreign powers could not agree on a division of China, was clear; thus it was thought best to uphold the fiction of an undivided China. Nothing that the foreigners have done to China has contributed as much as this deceit towards the decay of the Confucian ideas of the state and of the sacredness of the office of ruler. By it, they created a new criterion. Whoever could seize Peking acquired the recognition of the whole world as sole legitimate ruler of China. That suited Tsao Kun. The office of the headship of the empire conveyed to him no other idea beyond the amenities of the highest honours and unlimited wealth for himself and his. Tsao Kun was so avaricious that his generals were in constant and deep distress whenever it was a question of paying the troops. Wu Peifu paid his army in Loyang (Ho-Nan-Fu) almost exclusively with what he seized of the railway revenues and with levies on the people of the province of Ho-Nan. He was a man of strictly Confucian views and a perfect classical education. Even for modern war methods he did not care. Attack by infantry, led on many occasions in the first line by himself, remained to him the essence of warfare. Personal courage and discipline in his troops, however, brought him glory and victory over the other rulers in the empire. Feng Yuhsiang was a man of a similar cast. It is true, he was a Christian, and the foreigners called him the "Christian general." But in his utterances as a statesman he betrayed, at the time, a strictly Confucian attitude. In his army he enforced a strict discipline. In the streets of the city where he was stationed, the soldiers were admonished, from the walls of the houses and the arches in the city gates, by huge posters and pictures with Confucian sayings, to observe the traditional order. Tsao Kun and his two generals ruled over the north of China, from the great wall to the Yang-Tze-Kiang; though one must not take that too literally. For in the province of Shan-Si there had been, since 1911, the governor Yen Shishan who maintained his own troops and administered his province according to ideas of his own. Even in Shan-Tung there were more or less independent troops. But appearances were saved. South of the Yang-Tze-Kiang, in the province of Che-Kiang, ruled Lu Yunghsiang, who had his own views and leaned towards Sun Yatsen without being his declared follower. He was an old man and had grown up under the Confucian régime.

Nor must it be thought that these rulers were deadly enemies. They were opponents in a game; and the common circle of thought within which they moved united them. The old system of ancient China had raised them all aloft. All of them believed that nothing mattered but who would prove the strongest of all the "strong men"; once that was proved, a unified China would soon be restored. With a little acquaintance with western methods, the republican constitution, which was established after all, would soon continue the old bureaucracy, and happily so. No other did most of the foreigners in China think. Official attempts to bring the Chinese rulers together in a conference were not wanting on the part of the foreigners; they were to agree on the points in which

138

they differed, to divide the power among each other, and to restore a united, happy China.

Good intentions, these; but the outcome disappointed.

In the various camps there was a continual coming and going of middlemen. They conspired for each other, against each other; quality and quantity of the fighting forces decided for or against. Nobody wished absolutely for war. Dead soldiers and spent munitions did no longer weigh in the scales; a paper proof of power was sufficient. Where the question was of money and means, things became serious; money was the prerequisite for levying armies; and so for any position of power. In the fall of 1924 Tsao Kun's governor in Nanking claimed a rich district of the province of Che-Kiang. That claim led to war between the two provinces of Che-Kiang and Kiang-Su. As such things happen, big things followed in the wake of these little ones. Tsao Kun sent reinforcements from the north to Nanking. Chang Tzolin improved the opportunity and marched on Peking; he had an understanding with Sun Yatsen who was to assist Lu Yunghsiang. It was a chance for two parties to choke out a third party, by a temporary alliance. This knot of animosities was cut by the well-known coup d'état of Feng Yuhsiang. Instead of holding the city for Tsao Kun against Chang Tzolin, he seized the city, took his chief Tsao Kun prisoner, and drove his brother-in-arms Wu Peifu into the province of Hu-Pe.

This conduct of Feng Yuhsiang was a bad sample of how Christian ethics might work in Chinese practice of state. The expectations which the foreigners founded on the effect of Christianity on the developments in China were decisively disproved; and the praises sung in honour of the Christian general went silent at once. The conduct of the rulers in China, with which the whole liabilities of the Christian world were involved, was somehow a rather unchristian thing; and an asset was not easily derived from the only aim of these rulers, the aim to reunite China by blood and iron under the rule of the mandarins. That China of the rulers resembled the arena of a bull-fight rather than the field where a legitimate, democratic state power fought for its life against damnable anarchy. The people, so to speak, looked on from the grand-stand. One bull after the other braved the ring with blood-shot eyes. From a hidden gate issued a torero and dealt the death-blow, fair or foul. But the foreigners went on to hope all good things from a "strong man," if only he would show himself; and to fight wherever possible against the revolution of Sun Yatsen. The old things were upheld; and there was only watchful waiting to see to it that in the end the political movement of Sun Yatsen might not after all prove strong enough to enforce a change of front towards China.

But the progress of a cultural-political movement goes on quietly and under cover. Extraordinary moments of the coincidence of special circumstance are needed to make progress visible. Such circumstances had now arisen for Sun Yatsen's revolutionary moves. Feng Yuhsiang alone was not strong enough to stand out, in Peking, against Chang Tzolin. Between the latter and Sun Yatsen there was, at the time, a sort of political agreement; and generally speaking, the downfall of Tsao Kun had brought about an atmosphere of equality between the momentarily leading potentates. Thus it was easy to think of inviting Sun Yatsen to accept the position of the presidency. The greater part of the people considered Sun Yatsen, the founder of the republic, as the only man who had a real right to the presidency. Sun Yatsen, on his part, felt hampered by his position in the utmost south of China, while he wished to penetrate the whole empire; it promised a chance of success if he accepted the office of president of the old republic of the North.

Sun Yatsen entered Peking. Called by providence for the second time to the head of the empire, he saw himself for the second time near a realisation of his ideals. At this juncture, Death, with his hand of bone, interfered in the doings of men and took Sun Yatsen's life.

Well might truly loyal Chinese say with anxious expression, "The greatest man of our country is dead." In life-long self-sacrifice he had lived for the idea of his people—that idea which was to make the heavily laden millions freer in spite of all the rulers.

Sun Yatsen died. But his ideal for which he lived stands high and august before the eyes of the whole people and continues to act. Thousands and tens of thousands bowed down in mourning before the picture of the dead man and in reverence before the spirit of the man. In every spot of this great country and wherever on earth there are Chinese, that idea which he planted by his great faith and by his hard struggles has taken firm shape. Sun Yatsen, as Lenin is the saint of the Russians, is for all times the "great man" of the Chinese. For he has shown the people the freedom of self-determination; he has given the initial impulse towards a new rise of the Chinese consciousness, the momentum which will never rest, towards a reorganisation of the political and economic life of the Chinese continent.

III. THE CONSTITUTION OF THE NATIONALIST GOVERNMENT

MANY rumoured in China that Sun Yatsen's unexpected death had not been natural. There is no truth in it. Sun Yatsen was not well when he went to Peking. An abscess of the liver was suspected. German physicians performed an operation in Peking and found cancer; the case was hopeless. During his short illness the faithful followers of Sun Yatsen watched by the side of his bed. His wife and her sisters, the son, Sun Fo, the brothers-in-law, T. V. Soong and H. H. Kung, and Eugene Chen relieved each other in an unbroken watch in the sick-room. On one of the last days a Chinese physician administered a Chinese medicine which revived the sick man extraordinarily. Sun Yatsen admonished his followers to go on with his work. Especially did he place great hopes in T. V. Soong. The end came with a quiet burning out of the candle of life.

"Down from the flag-pole fluttered the five-coloured flag of the
revolution of 1911, the emblem of the republic . . ."

". . . and up rose the blue field with the sun of Sun Yatsen to
half-mast"

The people took the body from the house of death to the bier in the Outer Forbidden City. When the dignitaries of the old empire interred their emperor, the windows of the houses were closely hung; side-streets were barred with dark draperies. Not a glance of the people must offend the deathly quiet procession. But Sun Yatsen's coffin was accompanied by an immense crowd of people. Boy scouts opened the road through the throng. Boy and girl scholars brought wreaths; soldiers followed in military array; there were even peasants and workmen. The procession entered through the gate of the Forbidden City. Down from the flag-pole fluttered the five-coloured banner of the revolution of 1911, the emblem of the republic; and the blue field with the rising sun of Sun Yatsen rose to half-mast. Was it an omen, a warning to the people that the work was but half done? At the bier, the will of Sun Yatsen was read. Thousands and tens of thousands bowed before the picture of Sun Yatsen which looked down upon the coffin covered with flowers. A peasant in his old age, a general resplendent with gold lace, citizens, workmen, women, foreign diplomats, friends and foes passed by in an endless line.

After these solemnities the coffin of Sun Yatsen

was brought to a temporary rest in the western mountains near Peking. The Kuo-Mintang had resolved to erect a tomb at Nanking where the body was to be interred.

The result of the competition and the award of the prize for the most artistic drawing of the tomb were significant in more than one direction. The specifications called for a monumental building which was to hold the tomb in its interior and which would furnish, in the arrangement of the floor-plan, room for 10,000 people who might gather for festivities. A monumental approach to the main building over the hill which looked far away into the Yang-Tze valley where the tombs of the Ming dynasty are situated, was asked for. This competition was entered primarily by Chinese; but there were Germans and Russians, too. Paintings and architectonic designs were entered; there were a half hundred of entries from the whole of China, from Paris, New York, and other places. There was the massive, Romanesque architecture of a castle; the finely articulated tomb-style of western Europe, crowned by a dome and put together into an artistic whole with elegant Chinese ornamentation and Chinese terracings decorated with marble. If the

146

Chinese artist betrayed a fine feeling for the incorporation of western ground-plans into Chinese characteristics, models and plans for buildings in the Chinese style showed no less that Germans and Russians had mastered Chinese expression in architecture. Even a cubist plan had been entered by a Chinese. These bizarre forms screamed revolution into all the world. The first prize was awarded to a Chinese design. A building of the simplest Chinese spirit, in the austere style of the Sung dynasty, inserted in a park of arbor vitæ. This design was adopted for the execution.

Brief as Sun Yatsen's representative activity at Peking had been, it had not remained without bearing fruit. A meeting with Feng Yuhsiang had enlightened the latter with regard to the aims of the Kuo-Mintang and thus won a new friend for the cause of the people. Henceforth his army appears as Kuo Minchun (revolutionary army of the people). It is said that Feng Yuhsiang burst into tears at the news of Sun Yatsen's death. He is said to deplore the greatest loss of his life in having met this great man so late. The party centre of the Kuo-Mintang at Peking had been reinforced considerably; the schools and the university of Peking had been irresistibly invaded by the three revolutionary maxims of Sun Yatsen.

Of the leading personalities of the Canton district, only Eugene Chen had remained in Peking. The others after the death of their leader returned to Canton. Eugene Chen was to foster the association with Feng Yuhsiang; and above all organise the journalistic activities of the Kuo-Mintang in the north of China. This task came near being fatal to him. Feng Yuhsiang, after his insurrection, had not been able to maintain himself long as sole master of Peking; Tuan Shijui, accompanied by the troops of Chang Tzolin, had arrived and taken over again the office of Procurator of the Republic as if it went without saying. For a while it looked as if Feng Yuhsiang were going to fight for Peking. But he preferred to give way peacefully; and now he sat with his army in the inaccessible mountains of Kalgan. Herewith the field was left to Chang Tzolin. So, from the last struggles, his influence had emerged victorious. In the province of Chili, Li-Chinglin ruled as his faithful governor; and the province of Shan-Tung, under General Chang Chung Chang, soon took the side of Chang Tzolin. The power of the uncrowned king of Man-

GENERAL FENG YUHSIANG

The "Christian General." Formerly sub-commander of the president Tsao Kun, now commander-in-chief of the Kuo Minchun (revolutionary army of the people) and member of the central executive council of the Nationalist Government.

EUGENE CHEN

Minister of Foreign Affairs at
Canton and Hankau

churia overshadowed the provinces of Ho-Nan and Ngan-Hwei and thus extended to the Yang-Tze-Kiang. Only the province of Shan-Si maintained itself in the north in an independent balance. It was an inaccessible and needy mountain province. Wu Peifu had saved himself by withdrawing with his troops to the upper Yang-Tze; while on the lower river a new light had risen with General Sun Chuan-Fang. Lu Yunghsiang, the former governor of the province of Che-Kiang, as also Tsao Kun's governor of Nanking, had been engulfed by the last fight; and Sun Chuan-Fang had taken over their troops and the two provinces of Che-Kiang and Kiang-Su. In the midst of the rise to power in the north of Chang Tzolin, Eugene Chen fought the sword with the word. He has ever been a fearless champion. His attacks were sharp and stinging. When one day he launched the news of the sudden death of Chang Tzolin through the press, as a warning of the transitoriness of things in this world, the rage of Chang Tzolin knew no longer any bounds. Against all law, Eugene Chen was lifted from the security of the safe quarter of the foreign embassies and thrown into prison at Tien-Tsin. All the efforts of neutral politicians were needed to save him

149

from a military execution and ultimately to deliver him from prison.

That such things are possible is hard to understand for the European in his firmly built state. But in China they are significant of the power and the impotence alike of the military potentate. Everywhere in the empire there are the foreign reservations. In Tien-Tsin, Hankau, Shanghai, Canton, and in all the treaty ports, they are called foreign settlements (concessions); in Peking, the quarter of the embassies. There the foreigners had their own police and sometimes even troops. They had their own jurisdiction to which even the Chinese of these quarters were subject. To maintain this autonomy which the foreigners called exterritoriality and exjurisdiction, the foreigners had ordinarily to resist all meddling of Chinese authorities; they permitted no encroachments on the part of the Chinese police, or of Chinese troops, or of Chinese tribunals within the settlements. It might happen that the foreign authorities slept now and then beyond the grey of dawn: it did happen in the case of Eugene Chen: but only when their guests seemed to be dangerous to society because they were friends of the communists. Otherwise these settlements, with their foreign banks, were safe refuges for Chinese politicians and their money whenever things went wrong in China. There they could flee, to wait in safety for a turn in the tide; and meanwhile they could act upon China by means of conspiracy.

These conditions have often been criticised. Yet they formed only part of the background of impotence for militaristic rule in China. The chief cause of power and impotence alike lay deeper, of course, and in that rule itself. There was the caste of the old officials. From it had sprung all the "strong men"; to it all owed their power. Every official was a politician; every politician expected an office. At Peking they gathered; they courted the rulers; they haggled and intrigued for positions. There was an everlasting coming and going of officials from the provinces, of middlemen and agents; there was forging of plans and cunning machination of cliques. The rulers made use of these conspiracies in overturning their adversaries, in extending the reach of their power. They paid with high offices. Whoever could manage to place a sufficient clique of officials and military officers behind himself was to be reckoned with and claimed an independent command or a province; only to fall himself a victim to treachery as soon as an opponent of his clique had to offer more. That gang was an inexhaustible storage basin of cunning climbers; the one most devoid of conscience rose. Thus, often overnight, the old stars disappeared; in the morning a new name, never heard by men, shone in all the glory of power. Nobody was sure of his life for long; not Chang Tzolin, not Wu Peifu, nor Feng Yuhsiang. They all had their ups and downs, as the waves cast them on this surging sea of selfishness which was called Chinese politics or even the Chinese government.

The idea of the militaristic régime was the re-union of China under the bureaucracy. But where the only idea of government is thus torn and tattered by the policies of cliques, it is impossible that it retain a strength directed towards popular welfare. The people sank visibly into misery. The railways had been confiscated by soldiers. Soldiers took away the boats on rivers and canals. The produce of the country choked the thoroughfares; at all railway stations lay mountains of grain and seed and beans, given over to decay. Every campaign traced wide lanes of destruction of peasant life through the land. The peasant lad had nothing left but—to turn soldier.

But in the newspapers, not least in the foreign press, the praise was to be read of "the strong man." With every newly-rising star the expectation was voiced that now everything would be changed. They mistook the zeal for preparation and disciplinary measures in the army for statesmanship. To the realist machine guns and poison gas are ever a principle of state. But the poorest of all empires soon had the largest of all standing armies in the world: a million and a half men under arms; and as many robbers and pirates. Every skirmish left a legacy of stragglers and deserters to the poor. As in mediæval times, villages erected earthen walls around the dwellings to ward off the robbers. The peasants organised societies "of the red spear" and went out, with picks and forks, to slay soldiers wherever they could catch them. Within the walls of the cities, under the very eyes of the police and the troops of the "strong men," hair-raising mischief stalked. Shanghai, the foreign city, had every night its murder attended by robbery; and at least one kidnapping. When the ransom did not appear punctually at the secret place, the parents found, in the morning, the severed hands of their child before the door. Many rich Chinese did no longer dare to go abroad at Shanghai except with a bullet-proof corslet covering chest and back. Such corslets were offered for sale by foreign firms at Shanghai. Not all the warships of the foreign powers in Chinese waters deterred Chinese pirates from robbing coastwise craft. English steamers were taken by Chinese pirates, hidden, and robbed. Every other state, under such circumstances, would long since have perished in utter anarchy. The Confucian spirit, within the people of the old China, maintained the social structure even through such terrors. In the family, the oldest ruled; in the village community, the elder; everywhere, hunger. Together these upheld the inner order. As soon as a day of bearable quiet came, the people again went after its accustomed pursuits. It is a long-suffering people, of a great power of resistance in its family discipline and an inner order which never allows economic life to come to a standstill, in spite of all terrors and in spite of a murderous government. Trade and traffic survived in spite of all.

The foreign powers recognised but one government in China, this one. This government was a member of the League of Nations. The representative of this government sat as one of the judges in the commission which decided over the German-Polish plebiscite, over the national destiny of Upper Silesia.

The members of this government were often pliable before the foreign powers. They were well looked upon as rulers of China. At the great Washington conference of 1921 the powers made many resolutions of importance for China; among others for the disarmament of Japan and America in the Pacific. Of one thing—which would have earned them the enthusiastic and grateful following of an undivided Chinese people—namely of the disarmament of the military potentates in China, they did not think. The world, capitalistically organised, wanted to see China ruled by a power which on principle opposed a hostile front to that bolshevism which was coming out of Russia; the militarists in China did that. China was to be a bulwark for the colonial possessions of the western powers in Asia against bolshevism. They let it go at the now traditional, well-wishing policy with regard to the militarists and at a cold hostility for the Kuo-Mintang movement.

The leaders of the Kuo-Mintang now returned from Peking to Canton with the new knowledge that, for the renovation of a real government, the fight against "factors" in the result of the revolution of 1911 was insufficient. As president of the empire Sun Yatsen might have been able to gather the scattered elements of power in China for the purpose of realising his thesis of the three maxims of popular government. Sun Yatsen was dead. The Kuo-Mintang, with their aims, with their continuation of the work of Sun Yatsen, had fallen back into the great sea of the impotent people. A few individual leaders of the Kuo-Min-tang had gained the knowledge that the military rule and the conditions in the empire which followed in its wake had not arisen only by reason of the autocratic methods of single men; they understood at last that the transfer of the old hierarchy of office, at the time of the revolution of 1911, into the republican system of government had almost of necessity caused these phenomena to spring from the administrative system of the old empire. They found they were faced with the necessity of the decision to adopt new ways, altogether entirely independent of the revolution of 1911, if they wished to carry out the establishment of a popular government, promising success within the frame of the bequest of Sun Yatsen.

The unconditional power wielded by the highest organs of government over the army and the finances of an empire has, for western man, become inseparable from the very idea of suzerainty. It is for us what constitutes rule. Without it, there is no rule. In the old China, the Chinese emperor had, in this sense, neither been master of the army, nor had he disposed over a treasury into which all the revenues of the empire flowed. The country had been divided into provinces, provinces into departments and districts with officials ruling them who had been appointed by the emperor. The vice-roys had had royal power. Mostly they governed two provinces at a time; they imposed and levied taxes and duties; they maintained army and police; and they administered law and justice in their departments and districts. The emperor commanded; the servants of the empire obeyed. From every province the emperor demanded a certain amount of money which he ordered to be paid here or there; part for the imperial household, part for the relief of famine or as a subsidy for a poor province, part to be sent to foreign countries for the upkeep of embassies or the repayment of foreign loans, and so on. A budget of income and expenditure of the provinces the emperor did not know. The vice-roys imposed and levied the taxes through their officials in department or district; they paid the costs of administration; they maintained police and troops and tribunals out of these revenues and fulfilled the demands of the emperor. If riots broke out or if tributary tribes rose in rebellion along the borders of the empire, the emperor commanded a viceroy to suppress the disturbance. The emperor commanded; the servant obeyed. Not from an army or from money over which he disposed did the power of the emperor spring. *What preserved the empire for him was the power of faith.* Sovereignty and allegiance were founded on a religious belief in the order of heaven, on the belief of officials and people that, without loyalty to a God-given order, there can be no happiness for man; they were morality and religion of the Chinese under the old empire.

These sacred relations Sun Yatsen's revolution had no intention to destroy. Sun Yatsen believed in them; up to the day of his death he believed that they continued to exist; his spirit was part of their spirit. He followed the call to the presidency, he went to Peking among the wolves of the empire because he was led by the conviction that the spirit would conquer them. To live in great entities, makes a man great, and it embraces the world:

> Without freedom, what were Hellas?
> Without Hellas, what were the world?

The revolution of Sun Yatsen sprang from the very loyalty to the God-given order. But the onslaught of western materialism had done its work. As soon as the authority of the emperor had fallen, the authority of heaven also fell; an earthy spirit rose. It took possession of the order of state. Entrenched behind its own army, behind its own provincial revenues, independence raised its head within the divisions of the empire. Its very means of existence were withdrawn from the imperial court; the imperial government fell in arrears in the payment of foreign loans; the emperor was bankrupt. The Manchu dynasty fell. Now there would have been needed the leadership of a great man in China. Out of the independence of the provinces those many rulers climbed up, and with them civil war and disintegration. Does materialism know a great man? Materialism cried for a "strong man"; this cry found its echo. The "strong men" of material ambition prevented the erection of a new, united household of state; they were the cause of the popular failure of the revolution. The Chinese spirit died of democracy; the republic crumbled away.

The spirit alone has creative power. Materialism, a materialistic spirit is a sign of the old age of mankind.

Young China, leadership thinking in terms of creative power, *had* to turn away from standard democracy; for through the thinnest veil in which it drapes itself before public opinion they saw its naked reality.

Had not China for generations been moulded by the "sense of responsibility of the white man for the backward coloured nations" for the material purposes of democracy? With morally noble reasons the democracies had lured and driven backward China into the World War "for the protection of the freedom of weaker nations, for the right to self-determination of the peoples." Suddenly the Chinese saw themselves once more as a tool of the real aims, as executors of the verdict of annihilation passed against German competition in China. At the end, the treaty of victory dictated by the democracies at Versailles tore from them the province of Shan-Tung, in order to pay for the assistance of Japan in their war. That the foreigners also brought their achievements to China; whether or no Japan had won a right to her claims in the war; that ultimately, in the Washington conference, the province of Shan-Tung was restored to China—all that could no longer veil the nakedness of this reality.

Young China explored the history of democracy with a critical eye; it searched for the roots of reality. What had become of the French revolution, the prototype of their own movement? In the last resort it had lost itself in popular representation. From the solution matrix of a cultural entity the "rights of man" had crystallised out, precipitated in the vat of democracy as the freedom of the press, of speech, of assembly, and the popular franchise; they had hardened in a guarantee of the "fundamental rights" of the people. Its onslaught, coming from the deepest depth of popular demand, had been caught in the folds of the democratic cloak which capital had known how to throw over its shoulders. As a creative principle, nothing remained but capital.

With that a point of view had been gained which unveiled for China western realities; it showed up the materialistic movement in the work of the democracies of the nineteenth century.

Clearly it stood revealed how capital, through its task in the state, namely to finance the work of the poor, borne up on the arms of the very people, had created its capitalistic and industrial world. How the utmost endeavour in the interest of mechanistic achievement absorbed the spiritual strength of the people; how it whipped material passion on in the people; how it degraded its spirituality, down to what is dominant today in the soul of the people: cinema, radio, heroes of sport, boxer kings, machine guns, poison gas, silk stockings, and hats of velour.

A dissecting conscience went after the state mechanism of democracy.

Betrayed stood the universal but secret ballot as a cabal for the interdiction of the people in democracy. The people did not send its personally selected representatives into the government; it did not live politically in the life of the state. Paid politicians usurped its vote by means of an election according to parties and party lists; they left to the people only a gently but inescapably guided co-operation in a predetermined materialism of empire. Were not such cases significant where in America factories declared, on the occasions of presidential elections, that they would have to close down, for economic reasons, if this or that party came into power? Thus the feeling for justice is suppressed in the people and wholly turned away from the freedom of conviction. The bureaucratic state becomes a community of interests between bureaucrats and lawyers; stock companies become a bureaucracy of the mentally poor and the meek in spirit; and here as there insurmountable barriers are placed before independent intelligence. Is not higher education itself a privilege of him who has, with advancement blocked for those who are gifted and eager to learn? Technical achievements serve first of all the

162

creative power of capitalists; only five per cent of the population can afford a telephone. The poor who need labour-saving devices most cannot have them. A press dependent entirely on capital makes materialism the sole aim of endeavour, glorifying this life as it is in its great excellence.

Young China understood how the cloak of the democratic system, disguised as Christian morality, subjects to the materialistic powers which constitute its reality even a nation like the English people which is so little devoted to blind obedience, and so much to independent political judgment and to the brave sifting of right and wrong in national life; Young China turned away from standard democracy.

During the last years of co-operation with the Russian delegation Sun Yatsen had taken a decided bias towards the soviet state.

Young China went on in this direction. The idea that the conduct of the state was decisive for the elaboration of a common life and for the cultural development of the people was strong in Young China. Full of hope it turned to the new spirituality which came from Russia. It did not brag of a philanthropic heart, like western culture which meets the poverty of the people with Christian-capitalistic alms. This new spirituality clattered and clanked as it walked. By means of the hard fists of the poor, of the liberated power and creative urge of the common people, it meant to eradicate the neediness of the people. This fundamental idea of the soviet was identical with the dogmatic content of the thesis of Sun Yatsen which demanded that the new government constitute a new cultural community in which those who owned nothing took a decisive part. That other idea of Sun Yatsen's, too—to create an industry for "the benefit of the people"—was realised in the soviet state; just as it fulfilled the condition that the new government of China must rise from "the broadest mass of the people." In the soviet system the people elected the lowest organs of government; so that the foundation of the soviet edifice of state power corresponded to the municipal councils of self-governing districts. Thence arose, in the system as determined by Sun Yatsen, in an upward-tapering selection, determined by personality and ability, delegates to the higher levels of government. It was a building proceeding from below, from the people. On all the levels, legislative, executive, and jurisdiction remained undivided, as had always been the case in China; but no longer in the hands of mandarins, but in the offices of a direct representation of the people; their delegates appointed themselves all those powers which stood above them whom they could also recall.

By thus building from below, the new spirituality endowed the creative urge of the common people with power and authority. It created a system of government in which the popular spirit was supreme. Here Sun Yatsen's aim was realised in contrast to democratic popular government. The people did not elect at once the highest power of the state, parliament, in an anonymous count of votes, in order to fulfil as an obedient loose mass what the governing will of parties, politicians, lawyers, and bureaucrats decreed over it in the fight of parliamentary interests.

It had long been known that as a party the Kuo-Mintang might have created a political movement in the people, and that those officials, citizens, workmen, and peasants who were inscribed in the party lists of Sun Yatsen had given the party convention one significance, this: that they established the right of the people to search for the power of self-government; but with that the advance of the party system had come to an end. Here the new spirituality came in to help. It proved that ideas and slogans, thrown among the people by press and telegraph, uniformly from many centres controlled by a co-operative society, are more powerful than the influence of autocratic personalities or sectional interests. It was also evident that the federal principle which constituted unity in the soviet state, could more readily than anything else reunite the divided provinces.

The Kuo-Mintang, from a party, had to become a co-operative society of government, like the communistic party in Russia, and to develop into an executive group. That could be done by proclaiming the party convention as a national convention in the sense of Sun Yatsen's political bequest. A government of Kuo-Mintang members which based its power on the national convention would thus assume a national character and a national legitimacy for a realisation of the education of the people for self-government, and for an effective control over the army.

From this new spirituality, from an analysis in unbiased thought, of the things which made up a living present, arose the nationalist government of Young China at Canton.

The national convention of the revolutionary movement in Canton confirmed thirty-six members as a central executive council of the nationalist government.

166

This council, meeting every three months, became the supreme organ of government. It appointed, from its midst, the members of committees and councils in all other organs of government; and it recalled them. It ratified the legislative drafts of the committees and councils and acted as the highest authority in questions of party as well as the political and military affairs of the nationalist government. Nine of its members formed *a standing committee of the central executive council* which gave party decisions when the council was not in session.

Twenty-eight members of the central executive council formed the *executive committee of the nationalist government.*

It was its duty to act within the whole huge field of the social tasks of the government, for instance: peasant questions, labour questions, questions of trade and commerce, affairs of the movement of youth and women, public worship and jurisdiction, party organisation, and party propaganda, and settlements overseas.

The Standing Committee of the Central Executive Council, completed by six further members, became the *Political Council;* and nine military officers jointly with six civilians, formed the *Military Council.*

THE LEGACY OF SUN YATSEN

As executive managers, properly speaking, and facing the external world, five ministries were installed with five *Ministers* at their heads.

There must be, in Sun Yatsen's doctrine, a hopeful power. A little group of young people took upon itself the cross of the bitter hostility of the foreign powers and of the passive resistance to new thought inherent in the remainder of old China; returning to Canton to try to create the nationalist government out of nothing. Sun Yatsen had not been able to leave them anything with his political bequest but the power of attraction inherent in his ideas and clumsy beginnings of party centres in the empire, with, perhaps, a nucleus of political and military organisation, amounting to little enough, contained in the cadet school of Whang-Poa. The economic situation in Kwang-Tung was desperate; the military situation, full of dangers.

But the genius of Sun Yatsen steeled them for their task.

In word and picture his leadership was kept alive. Whenever school was opened, or a public meeting or session; early in the morning, on the drill field, before work began, for the purpose of hallowing every action, the bequest of Sun Yatsen was read. His picture adorned every room. Through the errors and mistakes of the day, his word led back to the victorious idea. Sun Yatsen's will spoke through his bequest; out of the tomb rose a unifying power which led upward. He gave a direction and an unconquerable aim to the hurly-burly of extreme, moderate, and opportunistic convictions which found themselves united in the central executive council. All the divergent convictions urged in directions of their own; it could not be otherwise. Right at the beginning, extreme-communistic inclinations declared themselves. They were fought and finally done away with by a piece of violence. Communism had never been the aim of Sun Yatsen. Political cleavage lines established themselves, a left wing and a right wing, each with its following in the party. There was a "clique of the crown-prince" behind Sun Fo, Sun Yatsen's son; an "uncle clique" behind T. V. Soong. The troops of the garrison of Canton believed at one time to be able to dictate to the new government. Extremes and conservatives joined in the defence against this worst pest which had arisen from the decay of the old empire. Chiang Kaishek led a night attack, surrounded the garrison, and, with the troops of the cadet school, forced it to surrender.

It was a difficult time, a chaotic beginning; but at last substantial worth asserted itself: those greater figures who served the will of Sun Yatsen most faithfully. At this juncture the Russian delegate Borodin did the impossible. He was the directing power; he inspired the spirit of discipline; he swung the whip of intellect which drove out the poor in thought over Shanghai where, in the party centre, a camp of so-called "conservatives" had formed. The knife-sharp objectivity of Borodin's political thought overthrew that intriguing pussy-footing which is characteristic of the Chinese politician of the old school; and thereby he procured for those energies which aim at matter-of-fact results a decisive victory. The effect was selective. Charmed by Borodin's character which was always sure of its aim, the manly elements among the Chinese gathered about him. They trusted and followed him; and they led their associates to adopt the same spirit. That gave the Russian officers and officials employed at Canton the courage for decisive action. It taught the government preparedness.

In the camp of the watchful foreigners there was much marvelling. Nobody had ever held a position like Borodin's among the Chinese; a position which permitted him to put his considerable abilities to such powerful use. There were doubts of its duration and of a real, lasting success. They knew their China.

Never had the foreign will achieved anything in China unless it had held the Chinese in line with the desired aims by a constant pressure, political or economic. Attempts had been made with the education abroad of Chinese youth and in foreign schools in China; also with the Christian spirit which the missions tried to spread. Everything had failed to give the Chinese continuity of a given impulse in the direction of a western European spirit of action, political or economic. Even personal guidance of the Chinese, by foreign teachers or counsellors, had long since proved to be a fatal illusion in politics, in trade and industry. The Chinese are full of mistrust for the foreigners and their guidance. Suspicion roots deep, deep down. The most proven friend is dogged, step by step, by a watchful eye, by an ever-prepared readiness to cause his downfall. That is a universal trait of the Chinese. It is born with them, arising from the high self-estimation of the culture of their fathers and from their hatred for the materialistic invasion of the foreigners into their tradition. The old, classical education qualified, within that arena of old China which was dominated by the spirit, for every office, that of an officer as well as that of an administrative official or politician. This old idea still remained in the new blood. It misleads the modern Chinese to attribute to himself powers which are bound to fail, because in the western sphere of materialism something is in demand which is not spiritual, namely a mechanistic power over things, a devotion to things, action, which he cannot give.

In the camp of the watchfully observing foreigners this spirit was known; and it was placed down in the account against Borodin. It was also known how corporative enterprise always went to pieces in China over the fight against intrigues and cliques. In the people, there was missing that matter-of-course submission to the service of a common cause, such as had been produced in western education by church and school, for the sake of co-operation within the whole national entity and for the sake of a socialisation of endeavour. The classical tradition of China did not go beyond the family unity; and outside of the old state which had become sacred by the will of God, there was no corporative discipline. In every enterprise of the community, whether it be a joint-stock company for the purpose of common profits, or a military or political enterprise, jealousies, envy, and slanderous suspicions rolled up at once and divided the whole into cliques. Secretive as is the nature of the Chinese, it was as if moles burrowed under the friendly, sun-warmed surface. Unexpectedly, here and there, the ground opened. The creative power of the best of them was crushed in attempts to bridge this decay; enterprise exhausted itself. The future of young China as a co-operative society could well be doubted. Yea, such a future had to be despaired of unless the new spirituality could bring a change even in such things. Some of the leaders were really above such intrigues. At times Chiang Kaishek was of these. That was his creative period. Always and on every occasion the transparent, simple, and objective characters of T. V. Soong and Eugene Chen were apparent. They were the pillars on which the bridge led over the abyss.

Two circumstances served as allies of Borodin. For one thing, the absence of any intention, as a matter of principle, of territorial or economic aggression, proved by Russia's voluntary abandonment of exterritoriality and exjurisdiction for her subjects in China, gave him a powerful protection against any suspicion that might be cast on his political aims. For another, his position as delegate to Moscow upheld

173

him firmly. Borodin did not belong to the diplomatic corps of Russia and was entirely independent of the Russian embassy of Karachan in Peking. He represented personally the co-operation of the world power Russia in rebuilding a new China. One thing was clear even to the most conservative hanger-on of the nationalist movement, namely that, without the menacing background of an allied Russia—which Borodin furnished—every step in the direction of national independence from the power of the foreigners must remain impeded. Imperative self-interest of the Chinese helped Borodin. But, in spite of all that, he could not command. No Chinese would, for any price, have suffered a foreigner within his ranks if he wanted to command; and within the nationalist movement the pride of absolute sovereignty was particularly pronounced. Chinese self-interest and the moral influence which Borodin's strong personality exerted though led imperceptibly towards a conquest of those obstacles which consisted in the passivity of the Chinese wherever a change of the traditional methods of government was contemplated. It was a thorny path which Borodin had to walk; for the disappointments which the Chinese know how to prepare for a passionate creative urge are heart-breaking. In thought and grasp they are past masters. But the more deeply the execution of an innovation had to penetrate the lower organs, the more certain was it to be absorbed by the passivity of the officials. Even Chinese leaders were only too often helpless. The next step was to co-ordinate Russian advisers in great numbers with Chinese officials. At times, sixty positions were held by Russians.

These Russian advisers had a great effect in training for readiness. Especially in the army did the influence of the new spirituality which they introduced into the ranks of the Chinese become apparent. A dauntless championship of the idea made its appearance. First of all did the troops of the cadet school of Whang-Poa, with brilliant courage, take the fortified walls of the city of Hwei-Cheu where Chen Chiuming's troops still lingered. A siege of two years came to an end by an assault. Chen Chiuming was disastrously beaten. Preparedness had already proved successful in that night attack on the garrison of Canton, thereby delivering the army of the nationalist government into the single hand of the chief-in-command of the government, General Chiang Kaishek. Now it drove Chen Chiuming out of the country beyond the seaport of Swatow. A brief campaign freed the province of Kwang-Tung of hostile invasion; for the first time the whole province was in the hands of the nationalist government.

These military successes made Chiang Kaishek the most-considered man in Canton. He was regarded as the head of the nationalist cause. In the end he believed it himself. In reality he owed everything to a willing and unconditional surrender to the inspiration of the Russians and to the authority which he procured for his military adviser General Galen and his collaborators in the task of reorganising the army. Another thing must not be forgotten: money. At this, his best time, General Chiang Kaishek admitted with simple truthfulness how much he owed to the silver bullets which the minister of finance, T. V. Soong, sent him into the field. Later he believed in nothing but himself.

At the time of the return from Peking, the government could count on nothing but the revenue accruing from the salt duties under the administration of T. V. Soong. Land taxes from the province rarely reached the treasury in Canton; the district officials had to live. The duties on tobacco, wine, opium, and gambling halls were unreliably organised; unimpeded smuggling made this revenue disappear wherever it was not seized by the military. A rental duty which had been introduced in Canton had already been levied for several years in advance; for currency there were only tokens. The issue of military notes had become entirely worthless; people refused to accept them; all bar silver had escaped to Hong Kong. No silver dollar was ever seen. The situation could not be more hopeless. At this time T. V. Soong wrote in a letter to a friend, "I have taken over the office of finance minister. I don't know yet what will have to be done; but there is nobody else among us who knows." One thing only was clear: finances had to be centralised. The consequences of the old fiscal system had since 1911 been apparent to all eyes. Administrative officials and military officers must not remain their own purveyors. They must be bound to the nationalist government by salaried employment.

The central executive council entrusted the minister of finance with a double task: on the one hand, imposition and levying of taxes and duties; on the other, the approbation of an expenditure by way of a budget, through a central bank in which all revenues of the empire were to be collected. A bold resolution; a task almost impossible of execution.

Income from the salt duties, considerably raised by

177

T. V. Soong's keen interference, had to take care of current expenditures as best it might. The military raised a threatening clamour. Divested of their power to levy money on the people wherever and whichever way it was possible, they were greatly indignant and often in real danger from mutinies. With escorts, heavily armed, they invaded Soong's offices. But T. V. Soong remained firm and fearless. Chiang Kaishek was on his side. It was in his interest to rob the generals of independent resources; the latter became thereby dependent on the command-in-chief. Step by step T. V. Soong took the collection of the revenues of state away from friend and enemy. His firm and fearless attitude, his transparent aim, his tact and persuasion did fully as much as the propaganda for the new spirituality in government. *He risked action.* He became the soul of the nationalist cause.

T. V. Soong was a banker. He had the instinct for business. He had that intuitive grasp of possibilities whereby economic creation rises out of fictitious substance. The financial conduct of Europe during the time after the war had yielded to him the secret of a paper economy, paper money, state paper and share paper. He understood that in a modern economy a budgetary balancing of the state household was sufficient to substantiate the fictitious value of paper money; to fund the debt of the state. Also private economy created a paper capital, he observed, and yet values to work with. Exchange of intrinsically fictitious wealth created a real national welfare. Such things could be done in China as well. T. V. Soong opened the central bank with printed bank notes.

The Chinese people knew only an economy of things. As in antiquity it still retained barter. Money was nothing but a metal, copper or silver or gold in bulk, coin to the full weight of its face value. Circulation of bank notes had been taken over from abroad; but not the fictitious valuation of the paper. From the moment when the exchange for the full value in metal, by the bank of issue, became doubtful, the notes were put out of circulation; their acceptance in barter was refused. T. V. Soong had thought of a means to circumvent this sovereignty of the people in their own economy, to eliminate it for a while. He decreed that all taxes were to be paid in his bank notes, and the issue of the notes was permitted only in exchange for coin. Five silver pieces of twenty cents against a dollar of the bank. Thus T. V. Soong created a silver reserve. Before the notes had, to any extent, assumed the part of a medium of exchange in the dealings of the Chinese, he had returned to a full protection of the notes in silver. At times these notes of the central bank, measured by the dollar of Hong Kong, stood above par.

That could not be achieved without any straining of taxation, without serious interference in economic life. Internal revenue stamps appeared on everything that was bought. Necessaries of the people were not spared. Coal oil, indispensable today to the Chinese, for illumination, had to pay its own value in taxes. Importers—the Standard Oil Company of America and the British Asiatic Petroleum Company —protested. According to the international tariff treaties with China they considered this extraordinary taxation as illegal; they struck. T. V. Soong installed a government control office for petrol and himself imported coal oil from Russia, levying the tax. Nothing could conquer him; he had the confidence of the people to back him. For now a new prosperity came. Shops filled with goods; money circulated. One thing the economic instinct of the minister of finance had discovered: high taxes did not hinder trade so long as the taxes were just and unconditionally and uniformly incident upon all classes. T. V. Soong gave trade protection against extortion; he restored the

T. V. SOONG

Minister of Finance in the Nationalist Government

GENERAL SUN CHUANFANG

Reactionary military ruler, one-time governor of the provinces of Che-Kiang and Kiang-Su; ally of Chang Tzolin

possibility of calculation for its transactions; with such securities brisk trade and even wealth which had escaped to Hong Kong returned.

At the end of 1925 the reporter of the British newspaper *North China Daily News* had to report that eighty per cent of the state revenue of the province of Kwang-Tung—up to four and a half million dollars monthly—reached the coffers of the minister of finance; and that there was a general prosperity in the province.

The nationalist government was constituted and consolidated.

WITHOUT any misgivings the thirtieth of May 1925 had appeared. Through the streets of Shanghai pulsed the usual life. As on every Saturday afternoon, innumerable people were taking their walk through Nanking Street. On the sidewalks, this way and that way, across the drive-way, coming and going, moved the crowds.

The Chinese are fond of such life in the streets. Whenever the grey concrete blocks, with their ten stories, at the lower end of the street, near the harbour, have been emptied of their thousands and tens of thousands of busy beings—when, in mile-long succession, the motor cars have rolled westward, towards the residential quarters of the city—when below the walls of Mammon quiet rules, then the Chinese people throngs broadly into the streets, to walk, to stare, and to talk. Into the background of the indigo-blue

182

frocks of the common people, there are mixed gay-coloured dots of the silken finery of women and children. Aimlessly the crowd pushes and idles past the gaily decorated show-windows of the shops. Hundreds of streamers, printed with advertisements, vie with each other from all windows in order to attract attention with their black, white, or gilt letterings. Through the wide-open doors there is a coming and going with tiny parcels tied with red string and filled with purchases; this throng which jostles itself good-naturedly has important business. Here someone stops marvelling, holding all others back; there a group recoils bewildered from the drive-way, like chickens scared by the horn of a car. It is a harmless, variegated life.

The foreign quarter of Shanghai has spread far and wide during the last decade. Never-sated, the sea of houses, barred in the east by the river, has swallowed up all open spaces in south and north, right up to the Chinese cities Nan-Tao and Chapei; westward it reaches into the Chinese landscape. Near the race-course, which stands now in the centre of the city, loom huge warehouses. With the fall of darkness departmental stores put on their vestments of light. Millions of bulbs illumine the contours of the outer walls, of the turrets and towers of these boastful buildings; they throw their glow against the sky and with their light-drowned windows make the street as bright as day. An arterial street crosses Nanking Street there, coming from the French city to the south. It connects, running at right-angles through the international settlement, the two Chinese cities of Shanghai: Nan-Tao and Chapei. Every now and then the stream of traffic —pedestrians, clanking street cars, motor cars, and rickshaws—must open up here in Nanking Street, arrested by a signal of blinking red and yellow lights, in order to allow the stream from south and north to pass. It is like a drum-beat in the rhythm of flowing life. A jerk seems to arrest the traffic from above and below. In the impatient jostling and the lurking hurry a gap opens up through which there is running and hurrying, past and through, with bells and blowings of horns.

At this point, on that unsuspecting afternoon of May, a procession of workmen and students appeared. They came on as a disorderly column, carrying white banners with Chinese inscriptions in their hands. It looked peaceful enough. Yet it was meant as a demonstration.

A few weeks ago, a Chinese peddler had been removed from a Japanese spinning factory in the foreign city—such a peddler as offers the workmen everywhere food, fruit, candy, and all sorts of things; they can be counted by the thousand; and the poor fellow had been injured; he had died—well, who would bother much about a coolie or anyone like him? Now these workmen and students carried on a demonstration on account of this mishap that had gone by without punishment. English policemen—the international settlement is governed by a municipal council in which the English have a majority and it is protected by British police—tried to disperse the procession as it turned into upper Nanking Street. There was resistance. The people in the street took sides with its compatriots. Traffic was held up; soon street cars were stopped in a jam; stones were thrown, God knows whence; the policemen had to retreat with their cudgels. Into a narrow blind alley, opening into Nanking Street at the Wing On department store, the multitude crowded after. At the end of the alley stands a police station. Seven years ago it had been stormed once before by the Chinese and totally dismantled. In front of the iron gate which had quickly been closed, the menacing crowd demanded the freedom of arrested students. The English chief of police was nearby in the race-course, playing golf. Already the riot had lasted quite awhile. But the chief did not take it tragically; he did not have time. More and more threatening did the situation become; they wanted to set the prisoners free. The guard appeared in the outer court, arms grounded. "Present arms! Fire!" No weakly consideration for this herd of common people who are in revolt against that will-to-power which is the general law of life! The shooting was sharp. Six remained behind, dead; seven were fatally injured and died in the hospital. How many more the crowd carried off when it dispersed has never been known.

Again millions of bulbs illumined the contours of the great stores, throwing a red glow against the sky; in the street where it is bright as daylight, the people walk about, looking and talking, the same evening, and the suburban resident drove to the theatre. Yet one could not but wonder why there was an armoured car standing at the corner where the arterial street from the French quarter crosses Nanking Street; why foreign "volunteers" patrolled the driveway; and why, near the race-course, a gun stood ready, four horses hitched to its trees. Perhaps it was nothing but an alarm for practice. Every nation has, at Shanghai, its volunteer corps, formed by the sons of the rich, for the protection of city and property. Since the World War there are no Germans any longer. They have no longer any exterritoriality or exjurisdiction in China; they stand under Chinese law. It is true that the British commander has approached the German community with the invitation to oppose the Chinese again in a martial way, now that the World War is over and everything is forgotten. But a German elder replied that Germany had disarmed. "Our young men refuse to carry the rifle." That was a reply dictated by policy.

The Sunday paper brought whole columns on the events of this unsuspecting Saturday afternoon; on Monday morning the doors of all Chinese shops were closed; the workmen were on strike; so were the servants of the foreigners; and in all circles there was a savage indignation against the British.

The whole chain of questions pending between Chinese and foreigners was unrolled. All classes in China had such questions pending. There were the unfulfilled promises of the Washington conference. There was the old demand of the Chinese propertied classes of Shanghai for a voice in the municipal council of the city; there was the categorical cry of the Kuo-

Mintang for an absolute sovereignty within their own country. In all these questions the whole of China stood solid against the foreigners. The Kuo-Mintang were backed in their attacks on the foreigners, not only by a united, but by an actively assenting China.

During the Washington conference of February 1922, it had been resolved that the foreign powers were to make a study of the state of the law in China so as to be able to propose to China such changes in the law and such reforms as might ultimately lead to a surrender of their exjurisdiction. Further, the powers had resolved to call a tariff conference to consult about the advisability of raising import duties from five to seven and one-half per cent of the value of the imports. And finally it had been resolved that Japan should surrender the colonial possessions of Germany in Shan-Tung which it had occupied during the War; and England, the expiring lease of Wei Hai Wei. The Japanese had done their part. There was the memory of a disastrous boycott on the part of the Chinese to induce them. The other promises had been postponed. France had procrastinated in ratifying the Washington agreement of the powers in order to arrive first of all at a favourable understanding with China as to whether the Boxer Indemnity was to be paid in worthless paper franks or in gold. Now a strike of the workmen in industries and harbour, supported by the Kuo-Mintang centres among the labour unions, with all the means of propaganda, recalled those promises. The rich middle class assisted the strike with large sums; the merchants declared a boycott against all British goods; huge protest meetings, and bloody encounters of Chinese propagandists with the English police spoke so unmistakable a language that tariff conference and exterritoriality conference met in a hurry at Peking. The powers could not allow matters to go any further. There was danger of German export firms getting the business; for German goods did not fall under the boycott. At Manchester, too, factories had to dismiss workmen on account of the failure of business in China; there were already too many unemployed in England.

Among the foreigners opinion was much divided. Many reasonable people admitted that China needed more revenue from the sea duties if it wanted to put its house in order. *It also needed a "strong man."* At Tien-Tsin where Chang Tzolin knew how to prevent every demonstration on the part of workmen, it did not come to a strike. Chang Tzolin took the hint and sent his Shan-Tung troops under General Chang

Chung Chang across the Yang-Tze-Kiang. He ignored the legitimate ruler of this part of the province Kiang-Su, General Sun Chuan-Fang, and occupied Shanghai.

Loud grew the anger of the righteous among the foreigners. Haven't we produced this flourishing city? Haven't we produced everything that thrives in a progressive way in China? With infinite patience, under privations, danger, and at the risk of our money, we have brought our goods, our science, our culture to China, not to mention the humanitarian institutions, schools, hospitals, churches; and now we are to surrender our rights, by way of thanks? We are to trust ourselves to a backward jurisdiction, our property to the impotent administration of the Chinese? As a matter of fact, the country was overrun by bandits and pirates. There was no strong central government which might have protected life and property. If the collection of the duties were handed over to the Chinese, the last security for the foreign loans was gone; and if the determination of the amounts of the duties were left to them, it might well be equivalent to the erection of a new "Chinese Wall" which would exclude foreign trade from China by its insurmountable height. All that was true from the

190

point of view of many foreigners in China. But their loudest clamour was directed against the terrorism of the workmen, against this bolshevism of students and scholars which was displayed everywhere and which demanded bloody deeds. If, on the one hand, the Kuo-Mintang spread its propaganda, with all means in their power, for the political and cultural aims of Sun Yatsen; on the other, the British press filled the hearts of the propertied classes with suspicion and fear of communism.

Meanwhile, under the auspices of the diplomatic corps, negotiations of the tariff conference were carried on with the government of Chang Tzolin at Peking. Here different points of view were dominant. The delegates kept their eyes on the larger economic and political interests. Japan sent sixty per cent of its total exports to China. It was to be feared that this trade the bulk of which consisted in the cheapest cotton goods would be killed by high import duties. On the other hand, Japan wished, by raising the tariff, to secure interest and amortisation of her loans to China. England and America were interested in the opening up of an extensive inland trade. If a considerable increase in the import duties freed the land of its transit duties in the interior (river duties), it might mean an increase in the total trade. They, too, were worried about their loans to China. The smaller powers, Italy and Belgium for instance, could readily agree to an increase of duties; their main interest consisted in a repayment of their investments in China. The Chinese agents held a very strong position. Behind them stood a nation stirred deeply by indignation; behind them stood strike and boycott. They demanded an unconditional autonomy in matters of the tariff. They submitted a new tariff, with duties of from seven and one-half to twenty-seven and one-half per cent; foreign products, from motor cars to wool and paper, were put down as luxuries and most highly taxed. When the Chinese get the chance once in awhile, they know how to demand. And they also know how to exploit the political situation. Behind a China united against the foreigners in this question of the tariff, Russian influence had a doubled power. The foreigners could not but fear that. The conference ended with the concession of a complete and unconditional autonomy in matters of tariff, beginning with January 1, 1929, and subject to ratification by the parliaments of the foreign powers.

Among the foreign merchants disappointment over this outcome was great. It showed in a unanimous front against the Chinese in the question of a Chinese participation in the municipal council of Shanghai. Here, too, the Chinese demanded the maximum of concessions. At Shanghai, in the international settlement, only foreign ratepayers have the municipal franchise. Rates are levied on real estate. The greater part of the real estate that is taxed belongs to the Chinese. They now demanded an equal franchise with the foreigners. The municipal council refused but conceded the election of three Chinese members against nine foreigners in the council. This the Chinese refused to accept. The old wound never healed and continues to smart.

For months on end Shanghai was in uproar. Volunteers and marines from the foreign warships in the harbour patrolled the streets day and night with armoured cars and machine guns. Business had stopped. Nothing much happened. What keeps the foreigners tense on such occasions is rather the knowledge of a smothered glow of which not much is seen on the outside, for the Chinese are secretive and passive, creating the feeling that no one knows what might happen. Without the newspapers which appeared every morning, most people would have known nothing of the smaller outbreaks of hatred against the foreigners which took place here and there in the huge city; nor of the attempts at organising demonstrations which were quickly suppressed. Slowly, as the official negotiations proceeded, while Chang Chung Chang's rifles enforced quiet among the Chinese, the usual life was resumed.

At Peking, the conference on exterritoriality was still in session. The Chinese demanded above all the abolition of exjurisdiction. It was naturally very unsatisfactory for the Chinese to be able to apprehend the foreigner only through a foreign consular tribunal; and then to have to accept a verdict given according to foreign law. There was little satisfaction in having a Chinese assistant judge present at the meetings of the consular tribunals. But for European ideas Chinese jurisdiction was very imperfect. Although a beginning had been made with a civil code after western models, and although there was a supreme court at Peking which for some years had been collecting pandects, use-and-wont predominated and a jurisdiction according to the personal feeling of the judge for what was right. Lawyer's pleas were not admissible; the judges themselves analysed the cases from the briefs. Legislation regarding commercial intercourse was very incomplete; there was no law of

194

exchange. The foreign merchant could not imagine how it should be possible to keep a complex apparatus of trade in good working order without these two prerequisites. Chinese custom, prescribing that the tribunal submit trade disputes—as interpretation of contracts, disputes about obligations of delivery or payment, insolvency, bankruptcy, etc.—to the guilds and chambers of commerce to pass on seemed to the foreigner to be conducive of procrastination and delay. The materialistic spirit of the West demanded in China conclusive verdicts of the courts of law, a written code from which the verdict issued mechanically, "ex machina" as it were, without consideration of purely human circumstances and destinies. Furthermore, that part of Chinese legislation which we should call criminal law was quite unacceptable to the foreigners. It provides for penalties which, according to western ideas, are quite out of proportion. Torture is still admissible for the purpose of determining fact. The death warrant takes horrible forms. Death by slow quartering is still known. Complicity of members of the family of the criminal may be punished by the extermination of the whole family, male and female, or by the castration of children and minors. There is death by decapitation with subsequent dis-

THE LEGACY OF SUN YATSEN

play of the head; there is death by strangling in a public place. These things were to be studied and investigated by the conference on exterritoriality. The delegates visited courts of law and prisons in many parts of the country. The Chinese did their best to make a good impression; but it remained no secret that jails and detention prisons were often in a state unworthy of man. The commission never finished its investigation; no report was published. A different, stronger hand was to anticipate its decision.

The political game for the influence over China, played between Soviet Russia and the western powers with a capitalistic organisation—a game which was hidden under all the negotiations—urged Feng Yuhsiang to action. Since he had met Sun Yatsen, he had had an understanding with Russia. Now, when a tangled knot united all China against the foreign powers, the time had come for a coup d'état. That knot which excited the people could be cut by the constitution of a soviet régime. Feng Yuhsiang marched down from his mountain refuge to seize the governmental institutions of Peking.

A game of chess was played by invisible hands of high politics. Only for moments were foreign inspirations heard in the war cry; only for moments

196

did foreign figures appear behind the movements of troops. Secret plans of Chang Tzolin were revealed to the people. "He wants to conquer the empire for his patrons in Manchuria, for the Japanese, to have himself proclaimed emperor." With this war cry Feng Yuhsiang marched on Peking, leading his popular army. Simultaneously Sun Chuan-Fang gathered the troops from the provinces of Che-Kiang and Kiang-Su in order to drive Chang Tzolin's general, Chang Chung Chang, out of Shanghai. The latter, however, did not accept a battle; as in flight he withdrew his troops across the Yang-Tze-Kiang into the province of Shan-Tung. Sun Chuan-Fang was master of Shanghai. The quick march of Feng Yuhsiang on Peking was a surprise. Soon he fought a sharp battle with Li Chinglin, governor of Chili for Chang Tzolin, with the possession of Tien-Tsin for a stake. Here, too, Feng Yuhsiang remained victorious. Li Chinglin fled into Shan-Tung; his scattered army tried to escape abroad, sharply pursued, along the railway from Tien-Tsin to Mukden, towards the great Chinese Wall. In such fights no ruler is sure of his followers. Chang Tzolin's general, Kuo Sunglin, who defended Shanhaikwan, the entrance through the Great Wall into Manchuria, deserted him. Chang

197

Tzolin's son Chang Hsueliang came hurriedly in order to intervene, without success. In very quiet corners it is being said that he himself was not disinclined to make common cause with Kuo Sunglin; it goes without saying, on payment of the highest price. Kuo Sunglin marched on Mukden without meeting with serious resistance, to the very gates of Mukden. Chang Tzolin's position was critical, yes, desperate; he prepared for flight. But his patrons did not desert him. Japanese troops occupied Mukden in order to protect Japanese property, so the papers said. An elegant flank movement of cavalry, inspired by Japanese strategy, caught Kuo Sunglin's army in a trap and scattered it; the dust of Manchuria covered two heads. Kuo Sunglin and his wife were executed. Chang Tzolin was saved.

The new year of 1926 saw then a quick return of Chang Tzolin to the old height of his military power. The rebellious troops were soon reunited under the general staff of Chang Tzolin. They were mercenaries. There were no political convictions, not even loyalty for a leader to overcome in the An-Kuo-Chun. These soldiers served for pay; a destitute country yielded them no other livelihood. Whoever paid them, him they followed as their master; never mind whether it were Kuo Sunglin or Chang Tzolin; never mind whether for or against the one or the other. An-Kuo-Chun: "The Army for the Restoration of Peace in the Country!" Thus these cohorts styled themselves. But the economic exploitation of Chang Tzolin, the false prosperity in the three outer provinces had received a death-blow. Chang Tzolin's Feng-Piau, a bank note by which he replaced silver in circulation, fell in value, became worthless. Chang Tzolin had tried to regulate economic conditions in the provinces by a word of command. Silver was withdrawn and replaced by the Feng-Piau. There was money enough in the country now; for awhile business flourished unusually. The foreigners praised the statesmanship of Chang Tzolin; for he paid for their deliveries of arms and munitions with the confiscated silver of the provinces. The bank of the central government at Mukden was closed; Chang Tzolin's institution, opened as a reserve bank, seized all metal. That was all very well so long as Chang Tzolin's power stood unshaken; but now it did not even help when Chang Tzolin had the money changers arrested in the streets and executed wherever they were convicted of depreciating the Feng-Piau. It did not help that Chang Tzolin forbade, on pain of arrest, to trade with Japa-

nese money, with the Yen. Everywhere there was a
flight to Japanese money; the Feng-Piau became
worthless; prosperity fled from the country. In
counting on it that the autocracy of the rulers would
sooner or later take care of itself, the Kuo-Mintang
did not count unskilfully. But it was a slow process;
it needed to be accelerated from the outside.

Feng Yuhsiang's popular army still stood in a
threatening attitude in the passes of Jehol (Tchong-
Toe); thence it was in a position to descend into the
plains of Manchuria. Chang Tzolin ordered the troops
of the province of Ho-Lung-Kiang to hurry down for
the purpose of relief. But here he met an unexpected
obstacle. The Chinese Eastern railway refused to
transport troops. It did not bow to the usual confiscation of the railway by the soldiers. It demanded payment in advance and, so far, ceased to operate. Since
Siberia had come under the soviet régime, this railway had passed from a Russian lease under a joint
Russo-Chinese administration. Chang Tzolin raved at
seeing himself thus frustrated in his own domain. He
ordered the military occupation of the railway. Russia
answered by concentrating troops along the border,
demanding in an ultimatum immediate and unconditional release of the railway. In the Japanese settle-

ment of Tshang Tshun, whole strings of Japanese transport cars appeared as if by magic. The world was faced with serious Russo-Chinese-Japanese entanglements. War stood before the door.

But war Russia did not want. Japan, too, needed peace. The Japanese Yen was still low since the great earthquake. For Russia as well as for Japan mutual peace was more important than the affairs in China. Chang Tzolin, wisely prompted by Japan, withdrew the confiscation of the Eastern railway. Feng Yuhsiang's popular army retreated to Kalgan; and Feng Yuhsiang himself laid down the command of the Kuo Minchun. He undertook a hurried trip to Moscow.

This move in the Chinese game of chess was finished. The counter move began.

The chess-men of the foreign powers stood in favourable positions. With Sun Chuan Fang's supremacy on the lower Yang-Tze-Kiang, a new soldier had entered the game: a militarist, an official of the old style and the purest water. Peking had been reentered by Chang Tzolin; on the upper Yang-Tze-Kiang, newly risen to military importance in Wu-Chang, stood Wu Peifu. He fought with his brother-in-arms Yang Sen for the province of Sze-Chuan.

The invisible hand reached out in order to arrange these figures for a far-reaching move against the bolshevist ideas of Feng Yuhsiang.

Middlemen, ex-missionaries, and interested Chinese intervened in order to smooth down the personal misunderstandings between Chang Tzolin and Wu Peifu. The prospect of financial help was powerful; for political convictions did not separate them.

The powers which could, through their consuls, determine municipal affairs in Shanghai held Sun Chuan Fang there. In this city, excitement of the Chinese population against the foreigners was stronger than anywhere else in the north of China. Events at Canton and Hong Kong threw their shadows on the wall. Sun Chuan Fang was invited to build a bridge for a renewed understanding between foreigners and Chinese. He entered the foreign settlement and delivered a gracious speech. He was enthusiastic about the technical achievements, the cleanliness and prosperity which the foreigners had introduced into the city, and asked his compatriots to emulate them. For this purpose, however, he also demanded the return of the rights which the foreigners had taken away from the Chinese.

Exterritoriality and exjurisdiction had taken a

special form in Shanghai. Apart from their character as matters of dispute between the Chinese and the foreigners, they held special possibilities. From year to year the overseas commerce of Shanghai had grown; the city had become larger; Shanghai was a seaport of world-wide importance. The far-sighted municipal council of the international settlement had to figure with that. It bought land from the Chinese peasants and built streets, telephone lines, power lines, and watermains for miles beyond the territory of the settlement proper, in the direction in which the city was advancing. Already large numbers of Europeans and Chinese had built along these streets. A residential quarter had arisen; the value of land had multiplied. But the Chinese looked angrily at the foreign police of the settlement which maintained order. They complained of the taxes which the foreigners levied on the owners of houses. These were encroachments upon the suzerainty of the Chinese state. There was no small satisfaction among the Chinese when Sun Chuan Fang was appointed, by the foreign authorities, to administer this "greater Shanghai." He was held in unusual respect. But not enough. The foreign powers protected even the rear of their new ally. One bright morning Shanghai awoke to read in the papers that even the jurisdiction in cases of foreigners against Chinese was quietly to be handed over to Sun Chuan Fang. Now it was time for the foreigners to get excited over their consuls. The most violent and not unfounded protests of the lawyers, otherwise so influential, made no impression. The foreign embassies at Peking confirmed the agreement of the consuls with Sun Chuan Fang whereby the exterritorial mixed tribunal of Shanghai had been delivered into the hands of the Chinese. Thereby a powerful Chinese court of law had been created. Foreign assistant judges had no longer any voice in the determination of the verdict; though they were still entitled to be present at the session; the consuls were directed to ratify every subpœna without delay, whether it was addressed to a Chinese or a foreigner in the settlement. Sacrifices had to be made. The ally had to be protected against attacks from the security of the settlement.

These sacrifices were not in vain. Among the three rulers an understanding was reached; the chess-men of the foreign powers stood aligned. Wu Peifu paid a visit to Chang Tzolin at headquarters. It was a chilly meeting of these two old enemies. Chang Tzolin was playing Mah Jong when Wu Peifu entered. "I beg my brother to drink tea," said Chang Tzolin; "I have excellent tea." With that the meeting was over. At once, however, there followed the joint attack against Feng Yuhsiang's Kuo Minchun in the mountain pass of Nankau, from June till August 1926. Chang Tzolin insisted on doing the greater part of the work. With the help of heavy guns and of most effective explosive shells, said to have been of Japanese origin, the pass was taken. The Kuo Minchun retreated beyond Kalgan, into Mongolia. It was not a disastrous defeat. In good order, with few losses of material and munitions, the Kuo Minchun reached new quarters on the Hoang-Ho, at Pau-Tu, in the Ordos desert. Then Feng Yuhsiang returned from Moscow, to resume his position at the head of the army.

If the foreign powers had counted on the formation of a coalition cabinet able to govern as a central government at Peking when they reconciled the three potentates, they were no less disappointed. The new W. W. Yen cabinet formed out of followers of Wu Peifu and Chang Tzolin remained an unsubstantial shadow. The inner sterility of the régime of the potentates frustrated the best-hatched plans for a reawakening of a reactionary China. Conciliatory construction was a thing foreign to the Chinese rulers.

Their power was not a creative power. With its hard onset of the will, the mailed fist merely tore the fine threads of a bond within the people, in politics and economics. Whoever, then, wished, like these foreign powers, to take hold of the order of the country, through this mailed fist, merely reached through the rents in the tissue of Chinese life into a void.

The outcome of this countermove of the foreign powers into nothingness was inevitable.

If the utter fruitlessness of a will acting through violence needed further demonstration, that demonstration was given by what happened at Wan-Hsien. In September 1926, two English freighters were anchored on the upper Yang-Tze-Kiang, before the city of Wan-Hsien. General Yang Sen, brother-in-arms of Wu Peifu, had requisitioned them, held them, and occupied them by force. In taking one of the ships, a mishap had occurred. A Chinese junk capsized; a few Chinese soldiers are said to have been drowned in the river. General Yang Sen considered the English officers as responsible and had them arrested on board. Against Yang Sen's stubborn will all negotiations and protests of the British consul of Chung-King remained without result. Two little British river gunboats steamed up the river in order to set their compatriots free. On board the freighters at Wan-Hsien everything seemed peaceful. Chinese soldiers were leaning over the railings, bowls of rice and chopsticks in their hands; the hatchways in the side of the vessel were open. On board the gunboats the landing crew made everything clear for boarding. They were received on the decks of the freighters by an infernal machine-gun fire proceeding from the darkness of the hold. With pistols and bayonets the British marines cleaned it out while rapid-fire guns of the gunboat spat iron on deck and silenced the Chinese artillery on shore which began to interfere. The officers arrested by General Yang Sen jumped overboard and swam for their freedom. An engineer was drowned; he was hit by a bullet while he was in the water and never reached the gunboat. The work was done; the prisoners had been freed. But still there was firing from the city. The guns of the gunboats answered. Having wrought destruction, the British force steamed downstream. A further expedition was to fetch the freighters. But it did not come to that; Yang Sen surrendered the ships of his own will. Without the foreign officers they were worthless for his troop-transports on the dangerous river.

How many poor Chinese, tied to the spot by what

little they owned, had to perish in the city, nobody knows. Great Britain lost seven young and brave lives. Such is the fruit which the stubborn power of the will bears for the nations: mothers must despair or, worse, must shed proud tears!

The Chinese have an old proverb: "Who refuses to kill a man, can rule the world." Sun Yatsen had held a great belief in this word. He had incessantly preached it to his people, giving it the weapon of co-operation in passive resistance against the superiority of the foreigners. The nationalist government at Canton knew how to use this weapon.

When news of the happenings at Shanghai on May 30, 1925, became known at Canton, the waves of indignation ran high. Mass meetings of protest were held. A giant demonstration against the foreigners was being prepared. English and French in the foreign settlement of Canton, on Shameen, were worried. Shameen is a little four-sided island. Two sides are washed by the river; on the two sides towards the Chinese city, a wide canal separates it from the main land. Formerly all foreigners lived on the island; but since the Germans had moved into the Chinese city, Dutch, American, and other business men had imitated their example. Shameen however remained the centre of the considerable trade of the British and French. The great foreign banks were there. Through the endless friction of the last few years irritation ran high among the foreigners on Shameen. They prepared a reception for the Chinese. From the warships on the river machine-gun squads and marine infantry were landed. The two bridges on the land side were barricaded with sand-bags; the windows of the houses boarded up. Now let the Chinese come!

They came on June 23, from the Chinese city, following the broad river street to Shameen: a variegated snake-line of men, drums, cymbals. Overhead fluttered the colours of Sun Yatsen and innumerable streamers with huge letterings: "Down with the one-sided foreign treaties! Satisfaction for May 30! Save China!" Uniformed soldiers, coolies, peasants, associations of employees, boy scouts, girl schools marched slowly up the street, a coloured snake-line in the midst of tens of thousands of spectators. At the bridge crossing to Shameen they turned in order to march along the city bank of the canal. A shot crashed. The whole front of the canal on Shameen spat fire. A panic seized the demonstration. Leaving behind their dead and wounded, and people who had been knocked down by sheer terror, the yellow "danger" dispersed in a moment, into the houses, into side streets opening up; the day had found its victims.

Who fired the first shot has never been found out. Was it fired? Did perhaps a rifle go off by mistake? Who knows? The massacre of a harmless demonstration had been done. Even though perhaps, after the general stampede, a few shots were fired from the houses of the Chinese city—it remained the massacre of a procession such as the workmen of Canton organise on every possible and impossible occasion. And Sun Yatsen's people seized his weapon. The consequence was a boycott of everything English, of everything that went under the English name.

A migration of Chinese followed, from Shameen and Hong Kong into the Chinese city of Canton. Servants, cooks, harbour coolies, factory hands, office clerks, merchants, all life and all trade fled to Canton. Shameen lay deserted like a graveyard; not a Chinese entered it henceforth. British ships in the harbour of Canton rocked in loneliness to the swell, shunned like the pest. Pickets of the strikers invaded every vessel in the harbour and confiscated or destroyed every piece of British goods. Armed pickets of workmen swarmed at night along the harbour and the river to prevent

the importation of food into Shameen and the British
ships. It came to this that not a ship, no matter of
what nation, could dare to anchor at Canton after
having even touched at Hong Kong. This boycott
lasted in undiminished strictness till October 1926—
for sixteen months. Thus Sun Yatsen's people conquered, by means of co-operation in passive resistance, machine guns and mortars: great, mighty
Britain.

At the time of the peace treaty of Nanking, in
1842, when England took possession of the colony
of Victoria (Hong Kong), it had been a bare, rocky
island without importance. Nothing but the bald
back of a mountain six hundred feet high rose from
the sea, separated from the south-east coast of the
province of Kwang-Tung by a deep-sea channel, aside
from the mouth of the Canton River. Hong Kong
was nothing but a poor fishermen's village, with a
spring of fresh water for the Chinese fishermen along
the rocky shore. Today the palace of the governor
overlooks from the height of the mountain-side a
huge city; from among green lawns, surrounded by
palm trees, peering forth from the shadow of giant
banyans. The strait is strewn with great ships. On the
far shore the clock of the railway station for Canton

gleams. Wide automobile roads wind up the mountain. Up to the summit stand stone houses; and for miles along the sea shore. The island is too small, today, for the enormous traffic. On the mainland side of the deep-sea channel which now serves as harbour, a second city, Kow-Loon, is grouped about the terminal of the railway. This territory of the province of Kwang-Tung the Chinese ceded to England about 1861. In 1898 it had grown too small and was enlarged by a further lease. In the two places there were ten thousand foreigners and four hundred and fifty thousand Chinese; up to fifty vessels a day came and went from and to all ports of the eastern and western world. At Hong Kong the goods of the oversea commerce of the whole coast of China were traded in, from Canton to Fu-Cheu. When at night the lights of the ships flared up in the harbour, like a reflection of the light-dusted mountain, then, in a literal sense, Hong Kong stood there, a shining monument of the enterprise and the creative power of the western world.

For sixteen months, from June 1925 to October 1926, the pulse of all this life had stopped to beat, The harbour was deserted. On the high seas the traffic of trade steamed past; for Hong Kong had no longer

GENERAL WU PEIFU

Reactionary military ruler in central China, one-time rival and
temporarily ally of Chang Tzolin

GENERAL YANG SEN

Reactionary military ruler in Sze-Chuan; brother-in-arms of Wu Peifu; responsible for the Wan-Hsien incident with British freighters

any busy Chinese hands which might unload the goods, and carry coal to stoke the fires of these foreign masters of technical progress till the boilers yielded their highest pressure. Only warships played against their anchor chains. But there was not even anything to shoot at. At Canton, it is true, the idea raged in the people in truly ugly fashion. The terrorism of the harbour hands was frightful. They invaded everything, often using violence. They tore the bales of goods open wherever they found them: in the ships, in the warehouses, in the street; and searched them for English wares. Much unlawful interference occurred. Foreigners were molested in the streets. The police never stirred. The Europeans became convinced that even the nationalist government was impotent to stop the rage of the strike committee. Carefully the idea on strike was kept from responding to attempts of the foreigners at provoking military action. There was to be no shooting.

One day an English landing crew from the British warships marched in and cleared out the head office of the strikers from the quay of the British River Navigation Company. No resistance was offered. The offices of the foreign customs remained untouched. Goods were seized in transit or in the streets. Yet it

213

THE LEGACY OF SUN YATSEN

had happened that goods had been taken from the ships, before they had passed inspection at the customs. That furnished the foreigners occasion to protest violently with the government. The foreign harbour authorities closed the harbour of Canton to all marine traffic. England threatened to blockade the river. Only then did the strike pickets cease from their encroachments.

Hong Kong meanwhile remained peaceful and deserted. The British government assisted the colony with large subsidies. But it could not prevent the morale from sinking lower and lower. Among the merchants' voices were heard advising to return the territory to China rather than to look on while the whole trade was being ruined. Property in land fell to less than half its former value. They were ready for sacrifices; they tried to negotiate with the government of Canton. The municipality of Hong Kong offered two million dollars if the strike were called off. The nationalist government was daily paying thirty thousand Canton-dollars to the strike committee; it asked for six million dollars from Hong Kong. That put an end to negotiation.

Public opinion of the foreigners in China held Russia responsible for the obstinacy of this fight. They saw in it nothing but the endeavours of Soviet Russia to injure the capitalistic nations in eastern Asia severely. Every foreign newspaper was full of slanderous news designed to arouse suspicion. A communistic conspiracy was alleged aiming at maintaining the population of Canton in an attitude hostile to the foreigners. Russians disguised as coolies were said to have fired the fatal shot of June 23, 1925,— that shot which brought about the massacre of so many harmless Chinese. According to British papers there was a communistic conspiracy which had challenged the slaughter of Chinese patriots not only in Canton but in Shanghai and Hankau as well. Germans can easily form a picture of this propaganda; they need only remember the years of war. That propaganda was kept up from June till the united front of the nationalist Kuo-Mintang went to pieces; it continues to this day. The foreigners believe that by such means they helped to bring about the disintegration of the Kuo-Mintang; and they are proud of it. But in reality England, which was the driving force behind that propaganda, did not quite understand what was going on in China. She fought against Russia in China from a dim feeling of fear really of a Chinese nationalist consolidation. The time is no longer far away when it will be understood that this attitude of the foreign powers in China was a mistake and against their own interests.

It was the Chinese themselves, not Russia, who wanted and waged the inexorable fight against Hong Kong. The nationalist government and the working people had, in that, acted on their own initiative. As a matter of fact, Borodin had for a year or longer urged them to call the strike off. The Russians are eminently practical politicians. Borodin had long seen that the extension of the strike could not appreciably help the nationalist cause; on the other hand, it meant a heavy liability in the budget. The money of the government should have been used for the inner elaboration of its rule and for the preparation of a campaign against the north. But Borodin's advice did not prevail.

Communistic ideas had taken very little root in China when the nationalist government established itself in Canton. There was no communistic propaganda worth speaking of in the nation. It is true that Sun Yatsen had received within the Kuo-Mintang certain communistic spirits. But it was done on condition that they should recognise the doctrine of Sun Yatsen and should not attempt to produce a cleavage within the organisation. Sun Yatsen approved of their opposition to militarism; and he feared that the militarists might rise to a dominant position within the Kuo-Mintang. The army was needed for the fight against the rulers of the north; but the opposing forces had to be organised as well, so that the power achieved might remain with the people and might not be usurped by the militarists in the party.

Borodin was, of course, a member of the communistic order of Russia. He belonged to the Trotzki group which is today known as the opposition of the Stalin government and represented, in Russia, the radical dictatorship of the proletariat. But to hurl communistic propaganda into the Chinese people was not Borodin's task. Trotzki himself has, on several occasions, issued public declarations of the aims of Russia in China. Russia, he said, gave its help for the purpose of freeing the country from the capitalistic compulsion of the foreign powers; it did not aim at a dictatorship of the proletariat. The proletariat of China had no political aims of its own. In the system of old China, its class had admission to the official careers; with this tradition the proletariat was satisfied; it had no desire to rule by dictatorship. The awakening of workmen and peasants to political life, by Sun Yatsen, had accordingly called forth, in labour unions and peasant associations, none but economic hopes. Here was a man who would help them to better themselves economically; him they followed. They had not risen to fight for power *over* the middle class and *over* the class of officialdom. In the Kuo-Mintang, too, and in the nationalist government, an overwhelming majority of members and leaders were totally averse to communism. They looked to the methods of Russia to help them lead the common people to salvation *themselves*. A dictatorship of the masses over their leadership they would not have tolerated; nor a communistic expropriation of private property.

Under these circumstances Borodin, communist as he was, had a very difficult task in the nationalist government. That he remained nevertheless an indispensable adviser for the Chinese, proves great power of will and an inexhaustible readiness to make sacrifices. Russian methods as such clashed often enough with Chinese ideas which are at bottom middle-class. A tragical conflict, for instance, arose about the organisation of the labour unions. According to the middle-class views imported from countries with a capitalistic organisation, labour unions are free institutions of workmen with the aim of pursuing common economic interests and a distinct policy of economic interests within the state. In the Russian political system there is no independence, no special policy of labour unions; the labour union is an integral part of the soviet state. The union is nationalised. It serves the government as a means to enforce the dictatorship of the communistic party and as a school for the education of labour in the philosophy of communism. Liao Chung-kai was labour leader in the nationalist government; he undertook and might have achieved the nationalisation of the Chinese labour unions in Canton after Russian models. The middle class fought him tooth and nail. At last he fell a victim to a paid gang. He was shot in the streets of Canton. That was an irremediable loss for the nationalist government. Even though the view of the foreigners that the government was impotent against the workmen, during the Hong Kong strike, is incorrect, yet the death of Liao Chungkai had this consequence that the government had to let the strike committee do as they pleased unless it was willing to use force. The strike degenerated into the lawless fury of an armed mob. Not until the strike against Hong Kong was about to be called off and the armed pickets were being enrolled in the army did the government succeed in giving the labour unions a legal form. The second national convention of the Kuo-Mintang, of 1926, declared the right to strike legal; and the central executive council carried a resolution whereby labour unions should henceforth move within the limits of statute law as passed by the government. To regulate all labour unions, a committee of the central executive council was formed. These resolutions had been dictated by the experience with unbridled labour.

The case was not as represented to the world by the British press, as if the Chinese, a red cloth over their eyes, had been driven into misfortune by the mystic power of a popular communist delusion. Every step towards a new state, rounded within itself, was an achievement in the struggle of the reactionary spirituality of the old China with the new Russian spirituality. What found a firm form in the legislation of the national convention was a doctrine of reality, a precipitation from the ferment of new political ideas in the people.

During the same national convention of 1926, the agrarian question was also answered legislatively. It was a hotly disputed question. It interfered much more deeply with the life of the people; and it was

more pregnant with consequences than the labour
question. Extortion of higher wages by the labour
movement had soon been absorbed by adaptive trade.
Higher costs were handed on to the consumer. Trade
and industry both had this remedy at their disposal.
Free private property absorbed the shocks of the economic struggle of labour, distributing its consequences
over the total of circulating capital in the country.
This purely economic fight did not affect the core of
life of the people. But the agrarian problem was a
fundamental problem. It concerned the whole economy of the nation and the existing culture. For that
reason this question was especially hotly disputed on
the part of the spirituality of the old China, opposed
to all communistic tendencies. A purely capitalistic
basis underlies in China only wholesale trade and industry; and these are prevailingly in the hands of the
foreigners. Native economics consists today, as it did
a hundred and fifty years ago in Europe, of retail
trade and small artisans. These again are very largely
fed by the rent which the toiler of the soil earns for
the owner of the land. Sixty, yes, seventy per cent of
the peasants are tenants. Fifty or sixty per cent of the
yield of the land is handed on to the propertied middle class in villages and cities. Thus the toiler of the

soil feeds the consuming middle class, and this in turn
gives work to native trade and native artisans. On the
other hand from this arose an enormous peasantry
held in slavery by poverty. They indeed were beasts
of burden, they did not even have the weapon of the
strike. They would succumb to hunger by whole families if they ceased to till even the least fertile soil.
Then though, in China, there can be no talk of capital—of the possession, on the large scale, of ready
money—in an economic sense, yet the whole of the
private property in the trading and artisan classes
took, from this circumstance, a capitalistic character.
It was tainted by the exploitation of a working population, and an expropriation of real property, its division among the tenants, such as Russian communism
had resorted to, suggested itself only too readily. But
the spirituality of the old China saw in that an immense danger. All circulating capital, so strongly
founded upon rents accruing from land, would at once
be driven into a crisis; the shock of the labour movement would then hit at agriculture without being
parried. From such an agrarian reform the Chinese
feared utter chaos. Still more, however, that spirituality of old China feared the consequences for the
state of civilisation. A division of the land was bound

to affect the family unit and to threaten its destruction. That would mean a death-blow to Confucian culture.

Here communistic endeavour met the most decisive resistance. Sun Yatsen had ever placed a high value on the existing family organisation. He had ever stood, with unhesitating determination, for the preservation of religious and Confucian statecraft. Seriously as Sun Yatsen tried to introduce Russian methods with their formal organisation for the settlement of the state; much as he wished to adopt Russian socialisation of the means of production and transportation, with the aim of making the wealth of the mines the wealth of the people, eliminating capitalistic avarice; and though, in a political sense, he sought an alliance with Russia; yet he declined, as a matter of principle, the cultural direction of Russian communism. The inner reorganisation of Chinese society, according to communistic rules current in Russia, he did not approve of. He revolted against an irreligious and rationalised philosophy of life. Economic elements were, in China, not to have an effect which would determine the character of its culture. True, Sun Yatsen had recognised that the weakness of the Chinese empire, as a united national group, lay in the family system. Family piety raised into a religious maxim had absorbed national consciousness. But following the example of the emperor Yao, in the ancient story, Sun Yatsen demanded, in the family state, a reawaking to the clan consciousness in the families scattered over all the provinces, and the organic consolidation of these clans, into a state unity. All that stood in contradiction to the circle of ideas within a communistic civilisation. It was an inner contradiction which divided the Chinese from communism; and the fight against the elements of the left, including the Russians, was fought inexorably. Wang Ching Wei, the first leader of the Chinese radicals in the Kuo-Mintang, had to resign his office as chairman of the central executive committee and go abroad. When it seemed as if the large number of Russian communists in the administrative positions of the nationalist government had a propagandist effect, in favour of Russian communism, among the officials, Chiang Kaishek surrounded the quarter of the Russians with his troops and machine guns and forced many to return to Russia. The consequence of all this was that the old-Chinese spirituality prevailed. The central executive council of the Kuo-Mintang limited itself to a reduction of the rental to be paid by the tenants to twenty-five per cent of the yield of the land.

That Borodin and General Galen—both Russians who stood above the average level of party members —could retain their positions throughout all these crises, proves that Trotzki's claim was true, that Russia did not aim at influencing China culturally nor desire to bring about a dictatorship of the proletariat or communistic expropriation in China.

General Galen accompanied the nationalist armies as chief of the general staff, when, in summer 1926, the march to the Yang-Tze-Kiang was begun.

During this year the spread of the nationalist movement had made great progress. The province of Kwang-Si had voluntarily united with Kwang-Tung. That was the first branch of the tree of the soviet republic. In the province of Hu-Nan the party centres of the Kuo-Mintang had planted the new idea among the people; the population was willing to surrender to the approaching troops of Chiang Kaishek with flying colours.

But the task of the minister of finance became ever heavier. The number of the officials whom he was to pay grew and grew. The army swallowed sixty per cent of the revenues. In spite of the fact that trade within the province of Kwang-Tung had developed considerably, that the coal oil monopoly had been abolished, and that even the foreign oil companies now furnished monthly considerable sums in payment of the excise duties, the minister of finance had to look about for increased income. The campaign against the north had to be financed.

So long as the sea duties were taken by the foreign powers, there remained for China, in the matter of taxes, a meagre field. Take the land tax. From time immemorial it had been low. Levied according to area, without consideration of the situation in village, city, or country, it was borne mostly by peasants. To increase it was impossible. The salt duty yielded already what could be expected. It depends on the consumption of salt which is fixed per capita of population. There were, further, provincial transit duties. But nobody knew better than T. V. Soong that these river tolls impeded and oppressed inland traffic. These duties had to be abolished as soon as possible. Add to that that the empire which rests on an economy of small trade, small craft, and tenant peasantry proved to be utterly unsuitable for the levy of a direct income tax. Other states in a similar position could resort to loans for the purpose of reorganisation. This road was barred to T. V. Soong. Domestic capital was unwilling to give money for the proletarian policies of the nationalist government; the foreign powers were the declared enemies of this government.

The only remedy possible for a new development of the state lay in the duties on imports and exports of the country. This source the foreigners held. Never was the submission to the foreign powers felt more bitterly. From passive indignation sprang active resolution. The nationalist government got ready for the decisive economic blow. It was backed by a more effective power than the Chinese politicians of Peking. It was backed by the people, by the unchained fury of the masses; and the news coming from the nationalist army, of the occupation of the Yang-Tze cities Wu-Chang and Hankau, stirred up courage in people and government to dare a bold stroke.

On September 23, 1926, Minister of Finance T. V. Soong, in the official *Canton Gazette,* called off the strike against Hong Kong and announced in its place a nationalist impost on all exports and imports of the province of Kwang-Tung.

There was no negotiation with the foreign powers in order to levy these duties of two and a half per cent. The people saw to it that no merchant refused to pay them voluntarily. No money could induce nationalist traders to accept goods from the warehouses of the foreigners unless a receipt for the Chinese sea duty accompanied them. Not a boat, not a coolie moved in the harbour for the transportation of export goods on which the Chinese sea duty had not been paid. The Chinese-nationalist associations of employees kept watch; not a warehouse, not a business escaped them.

The government had shot the nationalist spirit of the people like a torpedo against the sea duties of the foreigners. The financial control of the foreigners had sprung a leak. The Washington conference had been deposed.

V. THE MARCH TO THE YANG-TZE-KIANG

THE population of the province of Hu-Nan has a stubborn character. They have been known for that since time immemorial; and they are proud of it. As an outward sign of it, the people carry a blue cloth wound like a turban about the head. The custom dates from the time of the Manchus. When the Manchus conquered China, they forced the Chinese, as a sign of their submission, to shave the forepart of the head and to let the hair behind grow into a queue. The Hu-Nanese, in their stubbornness, wound the queue around their heads and covered it with a blue shawl. With the downfall of the Manchus, the queues, too, have fallen. But the Hu-Nanese retained their old head-covering which even today distinguishes them from other provincials. Their somewhat martial tradition says that their capital Chang-Sha was, during the Taiping rebellion, the only city which did not sur-

229

render to King Tsuen. The citizens defended their walls so bravely that the Taipings, on the march to the Yang-Tze-Kiang and to Nanking, had to leave them alone. In the revolution against the Manchus, too, Hu-Nanese troops fought at Wu-Chang against the imperials. The Hu-Nanese consider themselves the best soldiers in China. They speak a strongly southern dialect; and the neighbours in the provinces Hu-Pe and Sze-Chuan have mixed little with the mountaineers of Hu-Nan. Thus a provincial spirit is strongly developed. Since the revolution of 1911, the northern potentates have had to fight continually for Hu-Nan. The governors whom they installed in the province always found local rivals who did not hesi- tate to attack the northern troops of the invaders with their Hu-Nanese battalions. For a year now the Hu- Nanese general, Tang Shengchih, had been fighting with a governor of the province appointed by Wu Peifu for the power of governing the province. Bat- tles swayed this way and that way, without leading to a decision. Tang Shengchih asked help from the Canton government. He leaned on the party centre of the Kuo-Mintang in Hu-Nan and thus became their military nucleus. A convinced adherent of the doctrine of Sun Yatsen, Tang Shengchih was not. He was a mandarin, a military leader of the old school; he joined the nationalist movement because Wu Peifu would not let him rise. When Chiang Kaishek's troops approached from Kwang-Tung, the fight for the province was soon decided in favour of Tang Shengchih. The northern troops retreated from the province towards the Yang-Tze-Kiang and into the interior of the province of Kiang-Si. In the beginning of August the capital Chang-Sha surrendered to the Kuo-Mintang, and Tang Shengchih led the expedition on to the Yang-Tze-Kiang; while Chiang Kaishek commanded the operations through the province of Kiang-Si towards the Yang-Tze valley.

The rainy province of Hu-Nan had an unusually wet season. It rained in torrents. It rained as it can pour only in the subtropical summer of Hu-Nan. Disease tore huge holes into the ranks of Chiang Kaishek's troops. Dysentery demanded its victims. But high water in the mountain streams and floods in the valley bottoms permitted transportation by boats. Thus the march was greatly accelerated. The campaign was decidedly too fast for Wu Peifu. He was still in the north of the country, held by his co-operation in the Nankau pass against the army of Feng Yuhsiang, when Chiang Kaishek's men appeared on the Yang-Tze-Kiang. Where the Hsiang-Kiang, which, from Chang-Sha flows down the valley, joins the Yang-Tze-Kiang, the city of Yo-Cheu is situated. Here Wu Peifu's Hu-Pe troops stood guard. At Yo-Cheu many an inroad of Hu-Nanese into the province of Hu-Pe had been held up in years gone by. It was a good position on the hilly right bank of the Yang-Tze-Kiang. On this bulwark Wu Peifu relied. On the river, his warships were anchored in front of Yo-Cheu. But burning rafts which the nationalist vanguard sent down the rapid stream drove these watchdogs of Wu Peifu to flight. On shore a sharp fight was soon engaged. Here it was shown what is possible to the attack of a troop fired by an idea if it is led by a modern science of war. Neither disease in the ranks nor the privations of the long march nor the entire absence of support by artillery could deprive a sharp front attack of the nationalist infantry of a complete success. Wu Peifu's troops were routed. They fled by railway to Wu-Chang and by boat down the Yang-Tze-Kiang to Hanyang and Hankau. Before August had gone, Chiang Kaishek's troops stood before the walls of Wu-Chang.

Wu Peifu hastened to the rescue. He occupied quarters on board a Chinese warship on the river at

Hankau. From the anchorage both banks could be overlooked. To the right the yellow floods washed the foot of the walls of Wu-Chang. On the opposite side the river Han emptied out at right angles. On the right bank of the latter, the city of Hanyang filled the angle between the two rivers; on the left, the Chinese city of Hankau stretched away, its rows upon rows of houses reaching far up and down the Yang-Tze-Kiang. Both are open cities. Their walls had long since become too narrow for the great traffic which the foreigners had brought. They had been removed in order to make room for streets. Between Wu-Chang and these two commercial cities the Yang-Tze-Kiang, six hundred miles from its mouth in the Yellow Sea, is still a mile wide. During the summer months the largest ocean liners pass right up and moor alongside the foreign settlements which are located below the Chinese city of Hankau, along the river banks. The export products of the whole of central China are gathered at Hankau; and via the Yang-Tze-Kiang, the import goods of the West travel as far as the borders of Tibet; and via the Han inland as far as Turkestan. The railways to Peking and Chang-Sha make Hankau the distributing centre for the provinces of Ho-Nan and Hu-Nan. At the well-built stone wharf of the foreign settlements foreign warships lay in great number, ready to protect the palatial buildings of the foreign banks, the great export and import warehouses, and the customs office of the foreigners against the soldiery. Chiang Kaishek's troops had surrounded Wu-Chang; the city was being besieged. Above Hanyang, the nationalist troops crossed the Yang-Tze-Kiang, from the side of Wu-Chang to that of Hankau. Now Wu Peifu at last took energetic measures in order to restore order among his scattered battalions. A court-martial arrested the leaders of the troops that had fled. Shooting of officers and nationalist propagandists was in the day's work. Many who were innocent lost their lives. Blood-dripping discipline was to restore the lost position at no matter what cost. That is the only thought which military potentates can grasp in a crisis. But an idea that has begun to filter into the people cannot be shot. That was what Wu Peifu had to learn now; just as, during the past year, British policy had had to learn it through the massacres of Chinese patriots at Shanghai and Canton. Chiang Kaishek's troops were approaching Hanyang. This city holds the key position for the command over the three-city cluster. The decision was near. The na-

tionalist idea conquered. Wu Peifu's commander of
the city of Hankau deserted with his whole army to
the Kuo-Mintang. Forty thousand Hu-Pe troops
left Wu Peifu and marched up the Han. The part
which Wu Peifu could play along the Yang-Tze-
Kiang was at an end. With everything that he could
still gather of his army, he withdrew northward via
the railway. On the border between the two provinces
of Hu-Pe and Ho-Nan, he occupied a new position,
making his headquarters in Cheng-Cheu, the railway
crossing of the roads from Hankau to Peking and
from Hsu-Cheu to Loyang (Ho-Nan-Fu)—a strategically strong position whence he promised to return for the reconquest of Wu-Han.

Shut in at Wu-Chang, Wu Peifu had left two
brave generals who intended to defend the city to the
last man. They believed in a speedy relief by the Ho-
Nan troops of Wu Peifu; but the nationalists pursued Wu Peifu closely on his retreat and barred his
return from the north. Unspeakable sufferings visited
Wu Chang. The soldiers had requisitioned all food;
the citizens went hungry from the first day of the
siege. They caught the rats which, driven themselves
by hunger, issued from their holes. Soon even the
soldiers went hungry. On September 7, the city had

to surrender unconditionally; the nationalists entered and at once went to work to establish a soviet government for the province of Hu-Pe.

As a matter of principle, the military ruler along the lower Yang-Tze-Kiang, Sun Chuan-Fang, claimed the province of Kiang-Si as belonging within his domain. The governor ruling in Kiang-Si could therefore count on the help of Sun Chuan-Fang; and this circumstance had to be reckoned with when it came to a march of the nationalist troops into Kiang-Si. The campaign might easily have taken on larger dimensions than could be controlled. The more so since British diplomacy had just brought about a reconciliation of the three great rulers of the north. Wu Peifu and Chang Tzolin were operating together at the Nankau pass. It might happen that Sun Chuan-Fang and Wu Peifu united their fronts along the Yang-Tze-Kiang. To obviate that, the central executive council placed this restriction on Chiang Kaishek, not to extend the northern campaign into the domain of Sun Chuan-Fang, beyond the borders of Kiang-Si. The campaign was to appear as directed against the domain of Wu Peifu. In this stratagem the government counted on the unconquerable selfishness of the opponents. In order to save the power of Wu

Peifu, Sun Chuan-Fang was not going to make sacrifices. This proved to be no miscalculation.

At the city of Nan-Ngan the first nationalist troops crossed the border of Kiang-Si. They drove the Kiang-Si garrisons down the valley of the Kan towards the capital, Nan-Chang. At Ki-Ngan they met stiffer resistance; but it failed to arrest their march. When Chang-Sha had been taken, even troops under the personal command of Chiang Kaishek, coming from the province of Hu-Nan, crossed the border of Kiang-Si in order to advance down the Yu valley on the capital. An expeditionary force following the Siu River threatened the railway between Nan-Chang and Kiu-Kiang on the flank. With Chiang Kaishek was the staff of General Galen. This was the weakest spot in the alignment of the nationalist troops; here modern tactics were needed. Several times violent fights made victory doubtful. There were differences of opinion between the Russian general staff and stubborn underlings of Chiang Kaishek. These latter were often unable and unwilling to share the Russian wisdom, till a sharp reverse forced them to obey.

A high Chinese commander is often no more than what we are wont to imagine a mandarin is. A masterful conduct, the autocratic attitude of the armed man towards a helpless people, means military ways. This one or that one may, besides, be distinguished by personal courage; most are not. Very few have attended more than a Chinese military school or learned more than something of drill and tactics; they became generals, leaders of troops by reason of their high position in provincial office. Like all Chinese science, their military knowledge is derived from the classical books. Of modern weapons and their use they have the most fantastic ideas. Deeds and examples from ancient Chinese history give them something like a military tradition; and this mediæval tradition is their science of strategy. When the flank is threatened, the whole army falls back; that is a maxim. Whoever cannot hold the field, moves into a fortified position in the mountains or behind the walls of a city and waits for developments. Such is the war game of the Chinese generals. It is terrible only in its devastating effect on the people, in the destruction and exploitation of the country.

Through the superior tactics of the Russians the march of Chiang Kaishek became irresistible. Driven together from three sides, the Kiang-Si troops barricaded themselves behind the walls of Nan-Chang.

At Kiu-Kiang, on the Yang-Tze-Kiang, Sun

Chuan-Fang had meanwhile arrived with thirty thousand of his best troops from Nanking to defend his province. In the opinion of the old Chinese Kiu-Kiang was an ideal position. The left flank was protected by Po-Yang Lake; behind them was the river. From this strong position Sun Chuan-Fang commanded the railway to the capital Nan-Chang, which closed the third side of the acute angle between lake and river. It was a strong position which Sun Chuan-Fang held; so strong that, in view of the approaching nationalist armies, he could not leave it on any account in order to rescue Wu Peifu; Sun Chuan-Fang's affairs really became serious. Pushing forward from the Siu valley, the nationalists intercepted the railway. Nan-Chang was surrounded and besieged. The fall of the city could not be long delayed; a walled city is no longer what it used to be in the Middle Ages. The population of the Yang-Tze cities is many times what it used to be; nor do the cities live any longer by agriculture carried on within the walls. They have to rely on supplies brought in from the country; and troops counting by the tens of thousands eat up the stores of a city within a few days.

Wu-Chang had already fallen. Down the Yang-Tze-Kiang, on both banks, the nationalist troops of

Wu-Chang and Hankau were advancing against Kiu-Kiang. More and more Sun Chuan-Fang's strong position began to resemble a trap. But the city believed the enemy to be still far away. A surprise attack against the railway station awakened them. Batteries already were trained on the first houses; bullets fell among the thoughtlessly crowding people of Kiu-Kiang. Shots, fires, wounds received in the streets plunged the city into a wild panic. At the river front a munitions transport blew up. The nationalists had approached in the quiet of the harbour and laid the fire. Sun Chuan-Fang's steamer cast loose, head over heels, from the wharf and escaped. With a few of his nearest associates Sun Chuan-Fang got away. The army, thirty thousand men, was captured with all arms and munitions and enrolled in the nationalist forces.

The campaign was won.

On November 4, the capital Nan-Chang surrendered. Chiang Kaishek entered the city, fêted by the population like a redeemer. During the siege, suffering had been unspeakable. The people begged on their knees that the walls be dismantled; and, as a first act of popular government, Chiang Kaishek granted this demand.

In three months the nationalist movement had conquered three provinces. The impression which this success made in China was enormous. To the common people throughout the empire the symbol of the rising sun of Sun Yatsen became an imminent reality. Ready for action, insurrection stirred in the farthest provinces and flamed up in open revolt against the old system, against the officials who still opposed popular hopes.

Ngan-Hwei displayed the red flag. This province, reaching right across the middle Yang-Tze-Kiang, stood with its northern end under the shadow of Chang Chung Chang in Shan-Tung; on the southern bank of the river lay Sun Chuan-Fang's garrison. The people demanded provincial unity and independence from the potentates. Called and allured by the desire of the province to be included in the soviet system, the troops of Chiang Kaishek rolled down the bank of the river. The Ngan-Hwei garrison of the chief trading place, Wu-Hu, on the Yang-Tze-Kiang went over to the south. On the northern bank the peasants rose against the preparations of Chang Chung Chang for a counterattack on Chiang Kaishek at Kui Kiang. Their "red spear" societies developed a murderous activity. Nowhere was there safety against the peasants for the soldiers of Chang Chung Chang. In their quarters, on the march, everywhere they were surrounded. Whole troops were murdered in their sleep; not a straggler escaped death. Chang Chung Chang's march against the nationalists became an impossibility.

Even the province of Che-Kiang was ripe for a desertion from Sun Chuan-Fang's rule.

The province of Fu-Kien was taken by the garrison troops of Canton. General Chow-Yenjen represented there, as military governor, the rule of Sun Chuan-Fang. He allowed himself to be misled into a diversion against Kwang-Tung, the major part of the nationalist troops having left for the campaign against the north. But the garrison of Canton which had remained behind arrested his march; and on October 27, 1926, troops of the nationalist army in Kiang-Si also crossed the border of Fu-Kien, near Shau-Wu and Ting-Cheu. General Chow-Yenjen fled. During his flight he was slain by the peasants, with two hundred of his bodyguard. His severed head, carried about on a pike, was the gruesome sign of victory with which peasant gangs completed the surrender of the province to the nationalist cause.

At the same time the idea of joining spread in the

province of Yun-Nan. While Tang Chiyao, military governor and partisan of Wu Peifu in Yun-Nan, kept up the connection with the provinces of Kwei-Chau and Sze-Chuan, these three provinces of the upper Yang-Tze-Kiang formed a block of the old system which had stood out against the propaganda of Canton. The occupation of the province of Hu-Nan had, however, driven a wedge into this circle surrounding nationalist China in the interests of the northern rulers; for Kwei-Chau had gone over to the south. Already it was sending troops into the province of Sze-Chuan in order to drive General Yang Sen, an ally of Wu Peifu, from his position between Wan-Hsieng and Ichang on the Yang-Tze-Kiang. Thereupon the western part of Yun-Nan declared its independence of Tang Chiyao. It came to civil war within the province. Tang Chiyao was pushed from the capital towards the frontiers.

It went no better with General Yang Sen. A forced march to Chung-King saved him from destruction; but even there he could hold out against the people of Sze-Chuan only by pretending that he had been converted to the Kuo-Mintang.

In this mighty swelling of the nationalist cause the loss of Wu-Chang could not remain a mere reverse for Wu Peifu. His whole authority was shaken to the ground. Underlings in his army began to show that they had a will of their own. Inner quarrels among his followers, especially the opposition of many generals to the military governor of Wu Peifu in the province of Ho-Nan, forced him to gather about his person at Chong-Cheu the most faithful ones. The defence of the Ho-Nan border against Hu-Pe had to be left to two generals who were suspected of leanings towards the nationalists.

Henceforward ill fortune gave Wu Peifu no respite. Disastrous news from the province of Shen-Si supervened. There, General Liu Chenhua had been fighting for ten months to establish himself as military governor, a post to which he had been appointed by Wu Peifu. An ally of Feng Yuhsiang defended Hsingan, the provincial capital, against him. In this siege indescribable things took place. Even foreign missionaries were shut in for many months. They were spared the worst, however. They were granted free retreat from the city. Later it came to cannibalism in the city. Unexpectedly, on December 8, Liu Chenhua appeared at the headquarters of Wu Peifu, at Chong-Cheu, a beaten man. Feng Yuhsiang's relief of Hsingan had driven him from the province. His

MARSHAL CHANG TZOLIN

Uncrowned King of Manchuria, reactionary military ruler in the
north of China; master of the government at Peking

GENERAL CHANG CHUNG CHANG

Reactionary military ruler, follower of Chang Tzolin, commander of the Shan-Tung army of Chang Tzolin

troops were still holding out in the mountain fortress, Tung-Kwan, along the great road to Loyang, but called for immediate rescue. Wu Peifu's position was a terrible one. The quarrels among his generals prevented him from acting. His own general commanding at Loyang forbade, without ceremony, the approach of further troops of Wu Peifu's.

On September 17, 1926, Feng Yuhsiang, returned from Moscow, had resumed the command-in-chief of his old army, as a declared leader of the Kuo-Min-tang. By their retreat from the Nankau pass his Kuo Minchun had been practically dissolved. The greater part of the former army stood in the Ordos low-lands of the Hoang-Ho, partly in Pautu and Sar-Chi, partly at the opening in the Great Wall leading into the Ho-Tau district of the Ordos desert. Thirty thousand men had remained behind in the province of Shan-Si. The governor of Shan-Si, Yen Shishan, had seen himself forced to permit their settlement in Pauto-Chen. Other parts of the scattered Kuo Minchun Yen Shishan had enrolled in his own army. The new consolidation under the command-in-chief of Feng Yuhsiang gave the Kuo Minchun at once a new importance for the general policy of China. Since it overshadowed the territory of Yen Shishan, it had

245

become a danger for Chang Tzolin; for from the mountains of Shan-Si an invasion of the plains of Peking was possible via two great roads. Chang Tzolin mobilised his troops in the Sui-Yuan district against Shan-Si. But the plans of Feng Yuhsiang pointed in the opposite direction. He led his armies via Ninghsia and Lan-Cheu into the province of Kan-Su; and, having effected a junction with the troops of this province went on to relieve Hsingan and to attack Wu Peifu's flank in Ho-Nan. On December 15, 1926, Feng Yuhsiang drove the rear guard of General Liu Chenhua out of the border city of Tung-Kwan and marched against Loyang.

Chang Tzolin had a watchful eye on Wu Peifu's position. He could not allow Wu Peifu to be annihilated between Tang Shengchih, the temporary commander-in-chief of Chiang Kaishek's army in Hu-Pe, and Feng Yuhsiang. Otherwise it might mean that the nationalist movement would drive a breach into the whole existence of military potentates in the north. Chang Tzolin offered Wu Peifu the help of his Feng-Tien troops.

Wu Peifu's need was so great as to make him wish even for the two-edged sword of so doubtful a friend as Chang Tzolin. But his generals resisted. Three commanders of Ho-Nan troops threatened to leave the Wu Peifu connection. When, at the order of Chang Tzolin, nevertheless a few Shan-Tung divisions of General Chang Chung Chang marched from Hsu-Cheu to Kaifong, they were furiously attacked and driven back. In these fights Chang lost half of his white-Russian companies.

For a month Wu Peifu negotiated with his generals and tried to lessen the danger threatened by Chang Tzolin by stipulating the number and the position of the Feng-Tien troops at the front. But on February 10, 1927, Chang Tzolin, growing impatient, made a formal declaration of war, saying that he would now march against Hu-Pe and that he would fight against any general who would dare to resist him. In March the Feng-Tien troops crossed the Hoang-Ho in several places and entered the territory of Wu Peifu. Again the Ho-Nan troops took the offensive. Several times the invaders from the north were thrown back against the river in violent battles. Twice the capital Kaifong changed hands. Every defeat of the Feng-Tien troops called the "red spear" societies of the peasants into the field. A whole division of Chang Tzolin, ten thousand men, disappeared on such an occasion in the tenebrities of peasant revenge with all they carried. In spite of all, however, Chang Tzolin's forces advanced at last and occupied, on March 16, 1927, the railway junction of Chong-Cheu. The hostile Ho-Nan troops were driven back from the railway into the interior of the province, and disappeared in the country; though not without re-appearing later on.

The defence of the Ho-Nan frontier against General Tang Shengchih, commanding the nationalist army of Hankau, now fell to the united army of Feng-Tien troops and the loyal Ho-Nan troops of Wu Peifu.

West of Chong-Cheu, meanwhile, Feng Yuhsiang pursued his own aims. From his headquarters at Tung-Kwan he succeeded in winning over Wu Peifu's commander in Loyang. An attack unimpeded on this side disarmed the troops of Liu Chenhua and Wu Peifu east and west of Loyang; and suddenly the allied headquarters at Chong-Cheu were threatened from this side.

This strategic success of Feng Yuhsiang finally uprooted Wu Peifu. With a guard of not more than one thousand men he managed to escape and to unite himself with other troops. The Hu-Pe troops which, after the occupation of Wu-Chang, had marched up the Han River, and had found a refuge in Nan-Yang, in the western mountains of Ho-Nan. That refuge Wu Peifu now shared with them. But for the further development of things Wu Peifu, shut up in his remote mountain fastness, did not count any more.

Chang Tzolin, on his part, saw himself forced to try a quick decision in Ho-Nan. He proclaimed a general attack against Tang Shengchih in Hu-Pe. The offensive began during the last days of May 1927. The Feng-Tien army disposed of modern engines of war; and it was a mighty effort. Airplanes, bomb-throwers, even tanks were sent forward. There were many dead and wounded in the ranks of the nationalist army of Tang Shengchih. Yet the defeat of the troops of Chang Tzolin was inevitable. At the decisive moment the Ho-Nan troops forgot to attack. The right wing of Chang Tzolin had been entrusted to them. They at last went over to the nationalists. In complete disorder the Feng-Tien troops fell back towards the Hoang-Ho where a terrible fate awaited them. A large number of the fleeing army perished in crossing the river. Hundreds of them Chang Tzolin ordered shot on its banks, on account of cowardice and flight. In the water the headless bodies of victims of the "red spear" societies were jammed. The peasants slew the fugitives like cattle or threw them with hands and feet bound into the river to join those floating. Never had the Hoang-Ho seen scenes such as it saw on this 31st of May 1927.

Yang Yu-Ting, chief of the general staff of Chang Tzolin in Peking announced to the representatives of the press that a voluntary retreat, from Chong-Cheu as well as from Hsu-Cheu, had been ordered for strategic reasons. The attitude of governor Yen Shishan of Shan-Si could not be relied on, he said. And thus it appeared in the papers which announced further that Tang Shengchih and Feng Yuhsiang had effected a junction at Chong-Cheu on June 1. 1927.

This entire period from the occupation of the province of Hu-Nan by the nationalists stood in the sign of war and military leaders. The martial successes made the originally intended character of the campaign fade away. The defeat of potentates in the place of whose autocratic régime a popular government was to be established became more and more a campaign of conquest on the part of armed power.

When this phenomenon became apparent, no small anxiety was awakened in the central executive coun-

cil at Canton. That ostentatious limitation of the
powers of Chiang Kaishek, when he started for the
north, a limitation which forbade him to carry the
campaign beyond the borders of Kiang-Si, had not
only been a mere stratagem. It was also meant to prevent the very development of the war into a campaign
for the purpose of mere conquest. The revolutionary
aim of Sun Yatsen had not been the conquest of the
people by iron and blood, but its liberation; and it had
ever been one of the chief theses of Sun Yatsen that
the army should never be more than an *arm* of civil
government. As a matter of fact, the campaign had
been discussed long before it had been resolved upon
and the conservative idea of a slow progress from
province to province had purposely delayed it. It had
long been the prevailing intention to occupy first of
all the province of Yun-Nan and to organise it firmly
before the march northward was undertaken. It had
been the militarists who finally enforced the larger
enterprise when the situation in Hu-Nan demanded
an intervention of the nationalist government. The
danger which threatens in every popular revolution,
namely that its victorious military leaders usurp an
independent power of government—that danger the
executive council endeavoured indeed to eliminate by

appointing civilian commissaries for every army group. But this measure proved futile. When Chiang Kaishek and Tang Shengchih led the army to the Yang-Tze-Kiang, administration and finances of the province of Hu-Nan remained in the hands of military officers under their command.

The central executive council now resolved to follow the army. The capital was transferred to Hankau. The government of Kwang-Tung was handed over to provincial soviets; General Li Chaisam remained behind at the head of the provincial garrison.

On November 16, 1926, the government, with coffers and chests, started on the overland trip to Nan-Chang and Hankau. The journey resembled a triumphant procession. Everywhere the peasants assembled to greet "their" government representatives. Hope sprang up throughout the country.

The meeting with Chiang Kaishek at headquarters, at Nan-Chang, was cordial. Chiang Kaishek has always been held to be a loyal follower of Sun Yatsen; the civil government considered him as *their* man. All the difficulties which the Russian advisers of his general staff had had with his underlings seemed to be forgotten in the success of the campaign. The advance into the province of Che-Kiang was discussed;

it was stormily asked for by the general situation and by the attitude of the province. Chiang Kaishek delivered a flaming speech to the assembled people of the city of Nan-Chang. To the foreign powers in China he announced his determination to carry the victory of the word of Sun Yatsen, the liberation of the people from degrading fetters, throughout the empire and even beyond the borders of China. The power of conscience, coming from China, was to inflame the world against the will-to-power. Already there was a red glow smouldering under the territorial possessions of the foreigners in Asia. Kindled by the victory of the Chinese, in Java, in the Malay peninsula, in India, that flame was to consume the rule of compulsion over the peoples in the whole world. It was a Bolshevic speech.

At Hankau the arrival of the government was expected eagerly. There was an undercurrent of suppressed excitement in the masses of the Chinese city; among the workmen in the factories and harbour of the foreign settlement. The foreigners themselves looked forward with anxiety to what might happen; and like wild-fire the news spread on December 8, 1926, of the arrival of Sun Yatsen's widow who had come by airplane with T. V. Soong, the minister of finance; while the other members of the government were coming by steamer from Kiu-Kiang.

Under the eyes of the foreigners, an unwonted activity was at once displayed among the arrivals. The traditional distance which the old government had observed from the settlements remained disregarded; and even the reserve of the old officials who would deal with the foreign population only through official decrees fell down. The government secured first of all control over an independent American paper of Hankau and met the foreigners in English and directly. The old seat of government across the river, in Wu-Chang, was abandoned. There, only purely provincial offices remained. The minister of foreign affairs, Eugene Chen, in order to underline the suzerainty of his government even over the concessions, opened his office in the midst of the foreigners, in the former German settlement. Like two wedges the former German and Russian concessions entered the row of foreign settlements. The Japanese and the French settlements on the one hand, and the French and English settlements, on the other, were separated from each other by these two "exterritories." The former German and Russian settlements were called "exterritories" because they stood under a mixed,

Chinese-Foreign municipality, outside of the purely Chinese administration. That was a development induced by the World War; and the British had now reason enough to repent of their agitation during the War which had brought this breach in order to take away from their then enemies the last they had in China. In these two exterritories stood now the offices of the nationalist government. The ministers resided there, too; and their motor cars hurried henceforth through the quiet streets of the settlements. That brought an exciting feature as compared with the peace of olden times when the whole row of settlements had remained immune from Chinese political doings and when the foreigners had often looked on, from their balconies, with mild curiosity, at bloody fights on the far bank of the river.

Within their settlements, the foreigners had introduced no small discipline among the Chinese. Disorderly crowds, as they roll through the lanes of the Chinese city, were not tolerated. Beggars—that terrible element of misery in Chinese street life—gangs of unemployed, even portable kitchens so beloved by the coolie, but attended by choking smells, were banished. Coolies had to leave the sidewalks free for the better class of the public; the parks along the river bank were closed to them. Such a strict discipline and the really good pay which Chinese of the serving classes received at the hands of the foreigners had sifted out a thrifty gang of artisans and workmen for the concessions from among the order-loving of the Chinese. These people were contented. Life in the concessions was orderly and cleanly; and the settlements were a clear testimony to contented peace between Chinese and foreigners, rich and poor.

With the arrival of the new government came a high tide of political storms. In the Chinese city enormous popular meetings took place. From the speaker's platform words fluttered down over the hundreds of thousands of willing listeners—words of the "rights" of the working people, of an "abolition of tyranny," of a "betterment of the living conditions of the broad masses." There could be seen the unheard-of sight of foreign orators admonishing the Chinese to help themselves: a marvellous event the like of which had never taken place in Chinese history. These were Russian orators. Bloody revolution of Russian peasants and workmen against the masters and the well-to-do, things that dimly haunted Chinese heads—it all became clear as the light of day. The primitive brains of the coolies gave to these things the most primitive interpretation. The time had simply come for them to demand. Discipline in the foreign settlements was now tyranny to the coolies. Over the use of forbidden streets active quarrels arose with the police. The municipal council of the settlements did not wish to provoke anything; the rules were abolished. A giant procession now wound its way boldly into the very settlements. It crossed them peacefully and without being interfered with. But the next day brought the landing of British troops from the warships. Across the streets of the English settlement barricades sprang up. Excitement among the Chinese against the exceptional rules laid down for the concessions was not lessened by this measure.

In the French settlement, too, there were parapets of sand-bags and chevaux-de-frise in the streets. But the martial crews remained in invisible readiness. Thus it could happen that a troop of Chinese soldiers filed in full marching equipment along the French embankment. At the British barricade, a sentinel commanded them to halt. Hesitatingly, with defiant faces, visibly undecided whether to obey the call, the troop ceased to move. A moment of tense silence hushed the noise of the street. Then could be heard the snapping sound with which the cartridge slipped into the barrel of the British rifle. Death called. He passed. The Chinese turned into a side street off from British territory.

This situation in which the important business interests of the foreigners found themselves at Hankau made it impossible, as had been done at Canton, to ignore the nationalist government diplomatically. The foreign secretary of Britain, Chamberlain, gave up his uncompromising point of view whereby he would know only one government, the shadow cabinet of Peking. He now declared in the House of Commons that the British government might possibly find a way to enter into relations with regional power groups in China. The only thing that counts for diplomacy is to make a political move appear as powerful action. England, America, and Japan sent their diplomatic representatives to Hankau. Eugene Chen formulated his demands, as ever, clearly and unmistakably. He asked for the subordination of all concession territories under the sovereignty of the nationalist government. In the place of the exterritoriality of the foreign settlements he demanded a mixed, Chinese-foreign administration after the model of the already existing exterritories.

These negotiations brought no result. The demands

were too sudden for the diplomats. They departed without having achieved anything, but in the belief that they had pushed the conflict back on the usual track of negotiation. Public opinion in China though was such not to be satisfied. An expectant attitude is the way of a revolution; satisfaction is only in quick action. The Chinese got ready, not without having warned the British authorities confidentially, for a storm on the British settlement.

A bolshevist speech in the Chinese city by the minister of commerce Sun Fo released the arrow. Coolies, office clerks, workmen, all the common people poured from the Chinese city towards the entrance streets of the British settlement. The alluvial soil between embankment and water of the river offered a wide approach to the flank of the barricade. There, a line of British marines barred the way. At once they were tightly wedged in a coil of humanity. Blows hailed down; clods hit the faces of the sentinels. In the British consulate it must have been stormy weather at this hour. It is easily imagined that the British admiral raved when his blue boys had to take a whipping and dared not shoot. To shoot was against the command of the diplomats; and the British Consul Goffe was an intrepid defender of the clear knowledge that a massacre could end only in a disappearance of the settlement from the face of the earth. The admiral withdrew his crews on board the warships. The uproar poured into the streets of the settlement. Within an hour the barricades were trodden down as if they had been swept away. The mob scared the foreigners off the streets behind the locked doors of the houses. The chains of the cenotaph for the British fallen in the war were torn down; soon it bristled with revolutionary posters. They did not throw the monument over as the British patriots did with the German Iltis monument at Shanghai in the Great War. Chinese troops marched up and stood guard to keep order. They did not prevent the British police station from being demolished. The old police squad had fled. But there was no slaughter and bloodshed in this conquest of the British concession by the Chinese people. That was on January 3, 1927. Next day there was noiseless peace. Only an interminable Chinese crowd flooded through this reconquered piece of China.

The occupation of the British settlement in Kiu-Kiang did not proceed so decently. No attempt to defend themselves was undertaken by the foreigners. They had fled in time on board ship. Wild gangs of soldiers penetrated into the houses of the foreigners and demolished the furnishings. But even there no blood was shed.

Meanwhile the attitude of the Chinese against the British and in many cases against the Americans had, throughout central China, become very ugly and threatening; so that their governments gave the order to evacuate to their nationals. In the beginning of March 1927, there were no longer any British or American missionaries in the interior of the country; and women and children had departed from the settlements.

At Hankau there began extensive strikes of the workmen in harbour and factories. The secluded Chinese lower classes from the concessions became re-absorbed in the trade unions of the Chinese city. Even among the servants employed in the households of the foreigners a strike threatened to break out; in spite of the fact that these people were really well-off. The principle of organisation, on the part of the new government, took effect even where there was no real need. The demands of the union committees were extravagant. The right of dismissal was to be taken away entirely from the employers. Apart from unreasonable increases in wages they demanded a voice in the engagement, dismissal, and employment of workmen; and similar extravagant things. But the Chinese coolie and workman are at bottom reasonable people. They can see that exorbitant demands might deprive them of their livelihood. Here the Germans of Hankau offered meritorious mediation. Politically, they were considered harmless by the Chinese; for they possessed no longer any exceptional rights and stood under Chinese law. This enabled them to look at these questions as purely economic concerns. A German merchant managed to gather the various nationalities around the council table. Whenever intolerable demands were made, he negotiated indefatigably, in a friendly spirit, but firmly. A strong sense of justice spoke from his lips. Such an attitude is irresistible to the common labourer among the Chinese; the Confucian rule that it is contemptible to act against reason is too deeply engrained in his simple ways. After long-protracted negotiations which, according to Chinese custom, had often been broken off and resumed, agreements were reached between employers and labour unions which led industry and trade back into navigable channels.

The nationalist government has often been reproached, not only with bolshevist, but even with anarchist principles. The British press in China exhausted its resources in representing the labour-union movement among the workmen in foreign enterprises and the war against the exceptional rights of foreigners in China as a race war. How great the influence of this propaganda was, showed itself in the prejudice with which the foreigners in Hankau received the nationalist government. It was universally accepted as true that they wished to abolish all foreign trade. At the very least it was expected that Russian communism would break out, with all the terrors which this word has for a capitalistic imagination. All that was political propaganda. The leading men within the nationalist cause knew very well that foreign trade brought in a considerable part of the revenue of the state and that China had no other source of income from which it could derive money for the new needs. Even to the Chinese his skin is nearer than Russian accoutrements. The nationalist government wished to arrive with the foreign powers at a friendly regulation, by treaty, of the status of the concessions and of the foreigners in China. Eugene Chen, minister of foreign affairs, published, on January 25, 1927, in the *Hankau Herald,* a manifest in which he explained the fundamental views of his government. "In spite of its insistence on the demand for

263

Chinese sovereignty and in spite of a determined defence of national interests, the government will unconditionally respect the rights of foreigners and deal justice to them."

The word was followed by the deed. On February 19, the nationalist government signed an agreement with the diplomatic representative of Britain, O'Malley, whereby the British settlements of Hankau and Kiu-Kiang were placed, as Chinese exterritories, under a mixed Chinese-foreign administration; and whereby the Chinese government indemnified Britain for all the destruction at Kiu-Kiang.

HEADQUARTERS of the nationalist armies had remained at Nan-Chang when the councils were moved
to Hankau. Even Chiang Kaishek had remained behind. He was out of humour.

Negotiations at Nan-Chang, with the political
council present, had not gone according to Chiang
Kaishek's wishes. It had been resolved that the order
of the central executive council not to extend the
campaign beyond the borders of the province of
Kiang-Si should stand. The necessity to organise the
conquered territory and to get it firmly under the
control of the nationalist administration before extending the conquest was only too evident. So far the
province of Kwang-Tung had borne the cost of the
war. This source of revenue had been overdrawn. The
note issues of the central bank at Canton had swollen
alarmingly. It was imperative that the resources of

the conquered provinces should be made available and drawn upon. But Chiang Kaishek believed that, behind the indispensable measure, he could feel a secret sting. Many things worked together. He suspected a move of revenge on the part of Borodin. The shadow of that expulsion of Russian communists from Canton, in March of the previous year, still lay between them. If Chiang Kaishek, a son of the province of Che-Kiang, entered there as liberator and victor, the provincial spirit of the Chinese would ascribe to him a special weight within the nationalist government. That, Chiang Kaishek believed, Borodin wished to prevent. Besides, there was an evil spirit which stood behind Chiang Kaishek, whispering. His friend and adviser Chang Ching Kiang, a physically misformed man, a fanatic, fanned Chiang Kaishek's suspicions. In the circle of Chiang Kaishek's generals evil spirits whispered of an intention on the part of the Hankau soviets to raise General Tang Shengchih who had led the expedition against Hankau to the post of commander-in-chief. In addition, General Li Chaisam made a move towards civil power in Canton. Military leaders tried to enforce there military control over the civil organs of government. Secret news reached Hankau of a military conspiracy to seize the finances of Canton. As he had done even while Sun Yatsen was living whenever he could not have his will, Chiang Kaishek withdrew, in his hot-headed, well-known way, from all co-operation in the government by soviet. He remained at Nan-Chang. Then he demanded the removal of the capital from Hankau to Nan-Chang. If the long absence in the field had already disturbed the inner contact of Chiang Kaishek with the council, his withdrawal from Hankau destroyed the last community of views. The occupation of the British settlement by the action of independent proletarian masses widened the gulf between civil government and military leadership; it became a breach.

During the third week of January Chiang Kaishek went to Hankau. All the government offices had been decorated for his reception. In his honour flags were hoisted in the streets; and all the ministers and high officials greeted him solemnly as the victor in the campaign. But what, at Hankau, was still considered a difference of opinion easily bridged, revealed itself now as catastrophic. Chiang Kaishek brought his fist down on the table. He ordered the government to be moved to Nan-Chang, under the shadow of his rifles. He attacked Borodin personally in a violent way. The whole opposition of his generals to the Russian command, during the march against Nan-Chang, was brought on the carpet. Everything that others had done for the glorious rise of the cause and of Chiang Kaishek, everything that had given his army victory was forgotten. After two days Chiang Kaishek returned to Nan-Chang. The worst had happened.

The very thing had happened which Sun Yatsen had always called the danger which threatened his work. The militarists of his own party got ready to exploit the victory of the revolution.

At last Borodin had been overtaken by that terrible disappointment which no foreigner is spared who devotes himself unconditionally to the service of this people. The scene with Chiang Kaishek threw him down on the sick bed. General Galen withdrew to the solitude of a hospital. An English writer has somewhere written of the Chinese as of "a coarse people," quite incapable of gratitude. How the Chinese stand with regard to each other in this deep thing, what they themselves feel, is hard to say. Probably, what is treason to us, is to them only human nature. They escape it by never allowing themselves to be caught in unconditional devotion. Within the family, even with strangers, the Chinese are as a rule full of the frankest respect for friendship proved, or services of friendship received; they are touchingly loyal. Ingratitude arises from the system. The social structure of family ties withholds their innermost from flowing readily into the wider social connections. But is not in our own social, economic, and political system a service also priced most before it is rendered? Even in our world of politics, finance, and industry, there is a far way to the pure heights of gratitude for its own sake. From this insight Borodin might draw the strength to devote himself again, with an ironical smile, to his old activities in the interests of the Chinese. But another blow waited for him. Mrs. Borodin, engaged on a journey to Shanghai, in family matters, was arrested as a spy by the troops of Chang Tzolin at Pukeu; she was taken to Tsi-Nan-Fu, and later to Peking. For a long while there was fear for her life.

Chiang Kaishek looked for and found an aggressive adversary in the communistic group of the Kuo-Mintang. Under the leadership of the minister of justice, Hsu Chien, that group developed an energetic defence. Chiang Kaishek had to defend himself against the reproach of having deserted Sun Yatsen's doctrine, of having disregarded party discipline.

The strength of the communist group in the Kuo-

Mintang originally was not great. Scarcely a third of the central executive council leaned towards communistic theses, such as a dictatorship of the proletariat and expropriation of private property. The soviets had only one really communistic member, the Minister of Justice Hsu Chien. So far communism had not been influential. The demand to combine a collectivist form of society with governmental authority was generally considered as being fulfilled by the soviet system. Through the majority, through Borodin and the nationalist ministers, through the influence of Sun Yatsen's wife, the purely nationalist ideas had governed: the ideas of the liberation from autocracy, of the right to self-determination, of the right of peasants and workmen to a share in the government according to their productive contribution to the life of the people, and of the abolition of the power of money over living life. But now communistic tendencies found greater scope to unfold themselves. The communists had received a task in the government; they were needed for self-preservation against the militarists. From the strike and the boycott against Hong Kong, and not the least from the successes of the mob at Hankau, they had derived a great consciousness of their aggressive power. The militarists and the for-

eigners shivered before this danger to their special
interests.

Chiang Kaishek conducted a skilful defence. He
acted as if he felt wronged. He hurled now communistic indictments against the government at Hankau and gave hurried orders for the advance of his
army into the province of Che-Kiang.

Now the communists at Hankau had an easy task.
The common people there were roused and ready
for every bold stroke. The provincial soviets of
Hu-Pe had a bureau of propaganda at Wu-Chang
which had much remained uncontrolled in its activities
by the nationalist government at Hankau. Tank
Yentak had, with the help of a German communist,
introduced a certain amount of method into its work;
he gathered statistical material for the propaganda.
Into the brains of peasants and workmen he ham-
mered a realisation of their vast numbers and figures
demonstrating their misery and their consequent right
to dictatorship. These things remained not long without effect. The Minister of Justice issued new rules of
outright class jurisdiction to all tribunals of the nationalist domain. Like wildfire this knowledge of
a new law of the strong arm spread among the tenant
farmers. They picked up courage to break through

the immemorial barriers of possession. Striking examples of special jurisdiction roused them. Thus a small peasant from the Hankau district found a hearing in a high court of law. My neighbour, he pleaded, has so-and-so much land. He has so much land that he cannot work it himself. I, on the other hand, have so little that my family mostly goes hungry. I could work a few more acres if my neighbour would cede them to me. The peasant went home to his village with a government decree in his pocket directing that the neighbour should cede him a piece of land. Such propagandist jurisdiction had its effect. The peasants began to take the law into their own hands. In the province of Hu-Nan where, since the occupation, no progress had been made under the hands of the military towards a civil administration it came to wild compulsion of the propertied classes. The military régime did not much care. Conditions in the province were chaotic. At Hankau, the nationalist ministers made great efforts to stop the terrible state of affairs in Hu-Nan. Borodin himself, with a delegation of the government, started for the province. But the communistic action of the common people proved to be beyond control. General Tang Shengchih began to fear even for the continuance of his military supremacy. He gave orders to his sub-commander at Chang-Shah to act against the popular fury, arms in hand.

General Tang Shengchih was, since Chiang Kaishek's apostasy, the military pillar of the government of Hankau. His conflict with the communistic movement promised no good issue.

The fugitive missionaries from central China brought evil news. Everywhere the missionary establishments had been occupied and often plundered by the Chinese. The pupils of the schools had revolted; they demanded the surrender of the institutions and their direction by student soviets. The Christian character of the schools was to be abolished. Native Christians were threatened with persecution by the mob. In Yo-Cheu, on the Yang-Tze-Kiang, a Chinese Christian priest was slain. Not all these happenings had their origin in communistic agitation. It is true the nationalist government had also made its demands on the missions; and many an institution had had to be closed. Liberty of instruction was abolished. Schools had to submit to Chinese inspection and were forced to place instruction of the pupils in the doctrine of Sun Yatsen on their curriculum. The Christian church itself was never involved in the interference of the nationalist government though. Religious freedom was preserved. In this respect excesses sprang really from the intuitive belief of the population that the spread of Christianity served as a means to anchor the "Imperialism of the foreigners" in China. They also sprang from an inborn mistrust of the Chinese people for the ethical principles of Christianity. According to Confucian ideas, Christianity gives sufficient expression neither to filial reverence nor to loyalty to the law. The people found in Christian doctrine an undermining of these two pillars of Chinese morals and Chinese family cohesion. It revolted.

The foreigners at Shanghai were thoroughly alarmed by all this news from upriver. Coming attacks on these foreign settlements were feared, such as had taken place at Hankau and Kiu-Kiang. The foreign powers resolved to protect their property. Warships of all nations gathered in the harbour of Shanghai. England landed troops from Hong Kong, from the Indian colonies, and finally even from England in the international settlement. They moved into trenches and dugouts which were built opposite the open land west of the foreign city. Around the settlements barbed-wire entanglements were drawn. Airplanes circled through the air; black motor batteries rolled through the streets. Shanghai was armed, for the coming of the nationalists.

The neighbour province of Che-Kiang was in uproar. An extraordinarily strong movement for independence arose. The population wished to join the nationalist government as an autonomous soviet province. Along the Chien-Tang River stood, waiting but threatening, nationalist troops which had come from the province of Fu-Kien.

Sun Chuan Fang had already, in Nanking, lost his firm grip on the province of Che-Kiang. Just now he had had to suppress an open military revolt of the Che-Kiang troops under General Hsia Chao. In the interior of the province many regiments stood in a threatening attitude against Sun Chuan-Fang. All the garrisons were very insecure. But the province adjoins southern Kiang-Su with the cities of Shanghai and Nanking; Sun Chuan-Fang had to defend them. Systematically he began to remove the provincial troops from their positions and garrisons and to replace them by reliable regiments from the northern parts of the province of Kiang-Su. Thereby he exposed Nanking and Shanghai, and at this juncture Chang Tzolin's satrap, General Chang Chung Chang, crossed the Yang-Tze-Kiang with his Shan-Tung troops in order to occupy a position of rescue. He took command at Nanking. On the railway to Shanghai he had an armed train manœuvring, with a white-Russian crew; the Chinese cities of Shanghai, Chapei, and Nantao were entered by ten thousand northern troops, and put under martial law.

Now confidence was restored among the foreigners of Shanghai.

Under the hangman's axe of Chang Chung Chang no bolshevism would stir any longer in Chinese territory. Over the foreign city watched thirty-seven warships of foreign nations and twenty thousand British rifles. Doubts were voiced now of the probability of an approach at all of nationalist forces.

There was a rumour, it is true, that towards the end of January 1927, the first troops of Chiang Kaishek, coming from Nan-Chang, had reached the Chien-Tang River in Che-Kiang. Uncertain news was spread of an advance of nationalist detachments through the valleys which lead from Poyang Lake and along the river from the province of Ngan-Hwei to Che-Kiang. Nobody knew anything for certain. The last days of February arrived before the papers

"His picture adorned every room"

of Shanghai could report a fight which was said to have taken place on February 15, 1927, on the Chien-Tang River. There had been fighting along a sixty-mile front, from Chuki, via Tunglu, to Fonnschui. The nationalists had broken through the centre. On February 27, the wire announced the occupation of the provincial capital Hang-Cheu. From the coast garrisons of Won-Cheu, Tai-Cheu, and Ningpo, Sun Chuan Fang's men fled by steamer northward. Simultaneously it became known that General Bei Bosan, a commander of Sun Chuan-Fang's Kiang-Su troops, near Chi-Cheu, on the bank of the Yang-Tze-Kiang, had retreated in favor of the nationalists into the province of Ngan-Hwei.

At Shanghai surprise was great. But there were compensations. British papers reported almost enthusiastically a new trench position to which Sun Chuan-Fang had retired. The new front stretched from Kin-Shan on the sea, via Hu-Cheu and Jihsing on the Tai-Hu (Lake Su-Cheu) to Taiping on the Yang-Tze-Kiang. It placed an impenetrable girdle around the whole territory from Shanghai to Nanking. Chang Chung Chang's Shan-Tung men with their trench mortars and bomb throwers filled the gaps in Sun Chuan-Fang's lines. These positions were impregnable. Shanghai did not lose confidence in the famous rulers of the north.

Business lies fallow in Shanghai. Trading routes into the interior are intercepted, railway and shipping confiscated by Chinese armies. Incessantly troops come and go. The foreign city is at leisure so should it not devote itself to the military spectacle in the streets? Regimental music leading, European companies of all colours are marching by. All Shanghai is afoot. On Sundays there is a grand parade with fifes and drums. Papa and mamma go out with the children to the park. Two hundred long-fellows in bear cap and tiger pelt lined up. Two hundred white apron-pelts, drums and fifes in twelve-headed ranks, aligned as with a ruler, spring to life, parade past. Such is the pride and the boast of the foreign people. And it is a marvellous spring at Shanghai, that year, 1927! When, in the climate of Shanghai, the warm rays of spring have chased rain away, then, overnight, green shoots spring up in the monotonous, parched lawns of last summer. As if wakened by magic from melancholy dreams, the branches of shrubs and trees stretch out; buds open; within three days the world stands rejuvenated in fresh green. There is a lure to

278

drive out or to walk beyond the trenches of the settlement, into the open landscape. Such was it, a beautiful afternoon, on March 20, when peace was suddenly broken by shots. The nationalists were there.

The following night was a terror in the Chinese cities of Chapei and Nantao. Guerilla warfare raged through the narrow lanes. Into their dark hollows clattered machine guns. At the North Railway Station of Shanghai stood the armoured train. Its guns thundered into the night. All around, the houses caught the fire of the Cantonese; the whole neighbourhood went up in flames. The fire threw its light on skipping figures, black-frocks who seized arms and munitions. Labour leaders had left their refuge; the faithful ones were at work. They attacked the police stations and took their weapons. Whatever could be found of the northern troops was slaughtered. There was no organised resistance; for the famous rulers of the north had in time, and in all quietness, withdrawn the major part of their troops along the railway. The armoured train had been sacrificed as camouflage; its white-Russian crew defended itself to the last cartridge: then it surrendered. Nobody has ever heard of them again.

It was the work of the labourers, this conquest of

279

the Chinese cities of Shanghai. On March 20, no more than the vanguard of the nationalist army had arrived. When the main troops marched up in the days that followed, they found the labour unions in power. They had fortified their quarters and patrolled the streets in armed squads. They organised the strike and backed their demands on the employers now by force of arms. The foreign city had, by the strong military garrison, been saved from the terror of conquest. There can be no doubt but that the volunteer corps of the citizenry of Shanghai could never have protected the settlements against the fury of the unchained labour forces. Unimaginable destruction, which the nationalist government could only have regretted, had been prevented by the crushing number of British landing crews, without bloodshed. But these offered no protection against the agitation of the labour unions within the foreign city. Strikes, in the harbour, in the factories, even in the public services of street car, omnibus, and post office, began as soon as the Chinese cities had been occupied. The unions defied the closest supervision of all approaches to the foreign city. Their agents found admission. They succeeded even in the centre of the settlements in shooting down the foremen of the foreigners who were willing to work.

Where the wish is the father of the thought, consolation is not far away. The foreign press hoped for a speedy reconquest of Shanghai by the northern potentates. The papers announced that two hours by train from Shanghai, at Su-Cheu, northern troops were concentrating. On March 24, huge movements of troops from Pu-Keu to the Nanking side of the river were observed by the foreign warships at Nanking. Thirty thousand Shan-Tung troops of General Chang Chung Chang were stirring. Rumour said that a great battle was being fought against the nationalists west of Nanking; fully trusting to their safety, many foreigners had remained within that city. The potentates of the north were resolute; but resolute to move into safety at Ching-Kiang where the great canal from Peking empties into the river, to safety across the Yang-Tze-Kiang. Thirty thousand men had secretly retreated. When the first nationalist troops approached the walls of Nanking with a desultory fire, the last regular detachments of Chang Chung Chang took flight. The city was left in the hands of straggling remains of the northern army.

They were joined by a disorderly soldiery, by southern troops which arrived in scattered formations. Thus the foreigners were in evil plight. Marauding and plundering soldiers, shooting in all the streets, barred their retreat from the city. They gathered under the flag of the consulate. The mob surrounded them; every minute looked more threatening. At last the foreign warships in the harbour recognised the situation; a barrage directed by the marine guns against the surroundings of the refuge drove the assailants away; and under the protection of the fire from the warships a British-American landing crew came to the relief of the civilians. But the foreigners did not get on board the ships without victims. The English harbour physician had been killed; the English consul wounded. In the Japanese consulate, where two hundred Japanese had taken refuge, the losses had been more considerable.

The foreign press was full of flaming indignation. The most terrible details were sent from Shanghai into the world, rumours of the violation of white women and of unspeakable happenings in Nanking. The nationalist government at Hankau was greatly disconcerted. It was being accused, with all the material on which anyone could lay his hand, of setting afoot communistic crimes. The cry of the foreigners for military intervention on the part of the powers reached its highest pitch.

For years now the spectre of military intervention had been going around. That was the essence of the traditional attitude of the foreigners in China; public opinion in the foreign settlements refused to acknowledge a turn in the tide. It attacked its own diplomats violently on account of their weak attitude against the Chinese; it could not understand why the powers had not long ago stepped in with armed force against the Chinese usurpation of well-founded and firmly established rights. A determined propaganda began in order to induce the home governments of Britain, America, and Japan to act jointly and aggressively. Excitement of public opinion had risen into an ecstasy. The suicide of a Japanese officer gave this state of affairs a dramatic accent. With the morning signal to hoist the flag of the warships to the top of the mast this officer shot himself, the very leader of the detachment of marines who had relieved the Japanese consulate at Nanking. He refused to survive the unavenged stain on the flag of his country.

The foreign diplomats consulted about a joint note to the nationalist government dealing with the crime of Nanking. There was talk of sanctions. In Florida, the United States of America hastened the departure of further marine troops for China. For the second time the world stood at the eve of a war in which the Russian-Asiatic and the capitalistic-western hemispheres would clash.

At last the press bureau of the nationalist government woke up. It directed its counter move towards America. As a point of matter-of-fact correction it destroyed the impression that at Nanking there had been planned excesses. In the sacked consulate of Nanking a southern soldier's cap had been found, it was true; but in brotherly juxtaposition there had been found the cap of a soldier of Chang Chung Chang. These and similar corrections poured water on the excitement among the American people. Eugene Chen, minister of foreign affairs, assured the powers in his eloquent note of the willingness of his government to have the happenings at Nanking carefully investigated; he demanded a just verdict according to the true facts. His frank attitude did not fail to take effect in the White House at Washington. By a public speech President Coolidge destroyed every hope for a military intervention in China.

Once more the great reaper war had been averted.

284

The fury of the hatred of the foreigners now contracted into a crusade against communism. The slogan of the foreigners found its echo among the Chinese merchants of Shanghai. At bottom they, too, had been infected by the idea of a soviet structure of the state. The Chinese of the foreign city did not hoist their nationalist flags above their houses entirely without inner conviction. The principle of provincial autonomy within a soviet state lured them; and they assented unanimously to the defence against the foreigners. But the usurpation of a commanding position in the state by the proletariat remained hateful to them. There were also quite a few conflicts within the families of the rich Chinese merchants of Shanghai which did their share. Parents who had grown rich could not understand why the younger generation within their own ranks should stake everything they had gained for the sake of an indiscriminate liberation of the common people. The propertied class among the Chinese joined its voice in the outcry against communism; and the unanimity of public opinion within those classes which disposed over capital had a great influence on the further course of events. Chiang Kaishek was visibly and powerfully influenced by it in his resolutions. From the now precise declaration of war on the part of the international propertied classes it became increasingly clear that they would recede from a repudiation, as a matter of principle, of a nationalist régime and this, at the very moment, but no sooner, at which that government promised to observe one point, namely the inexorable repression of any claim to power on the part of the common people.

This point was the innermost causal motive of the quarrels which had driven Chiang Kaishek into the opposition. He was a soldier. Discipline and order were second nature to him; he hated the phenomena of high-handed action which, against the rigid ideas regarding property held by the upper strata of the population, were necessarily connected with the emancipation of peasants and workmen. These fought against his military power. None but the straight communists among the members of the government approved of them any more than did Chiang Kaishek, but by the government they were regarded as transient, as not inherent in the system but incidental to the establishment of the system. This view was foreign to Chiang Kaishek's nature. To him, these disturbances were intentional anarchy; he held the communistic elements in the government responsible for them.

From such purely subjective suppositions Chiang Kaishek believed, no doubt in all honesty of conviction, that the right to strike and similar means of compulsion in the hand of proletarians must become fatal to empire and people. He believed that he was called upon, by means of the power of his army, to return the carrying-out of reforms to the hands of government. He wished to help the common people. He wished to concede to it the consideration which it demanded, but not the power. Self-help of the people he condemned as a matter of principle; and at last he went so far as to suppress it by force of arms. He had, then, reached the point where the reactionary propertied classes wanted to see the nationalist government.

Sun Yatsen had not only demanded the right of the people but also a sufficient measure of power for the people. All the members of the government at Hankau took this stand, with the exception of a few generals. The communists represented it in their radical methods, the moderates in more conservative methods of procedure.

287

Throughout the campaign in Che-Kiang and Kiang-Su the quarrel between Chiang Kaishek and the government at Hankau was carried on in the broad light of publicity. As is the rule in such cases, polemics were not concerned with the essential point but with such points of disagreement as were carelessly thrown out for the moment. The communistic group accused Chiang Kaishek of Napoleonic ambitions; he replied by indicting the whole government corporation of Hankau for communistic activities. With that he played the game of the foreign papers against Hankau. In spite of all that, however, Chiang Kaishek's speeches made a strong impression of honesty of character and of his own readiness to submit to discipline. He never ceased to repeat that he recognised the central executive council of the party as the highest authority and that he was willing to submit to it. He even approved of resolutions which deprived him of the leading position in the soviets. At Hankau there was indignant anger against the deputy president of the central executive council, Chang Ching Kiang, that evil spirit who, from behind Chiang Kaishek's shoulder, cunningly kindled disagreement. Chiang Kaishek himself went so far as to take a step of self-humiliation by recalling from exile Wang

288

Chingwei whom he himself had driven out in order to take again the chairmanship of the central executive council.

In the sense, then, of the old, classical bureaucratic tradition, Chiang Kaishek's attitude was irreproachable. But in his subjectivistic choice of position he committed grave errors against Sun Yatsen's cause. The collectivist system of government demanded of the nationalists first of all and under all circumstances, the preservation of an unbroken front towards the outer world. Chiang Kaishek, however, never redeemed his first step towards a separation, that step which held him at Nan-Chang. Holding on to his old stubbornness, he refused to attend the convention of the central executive council at Hankau which was called, as an emergency measure to save, if possible, the régime at Hankau out of dissension, for the date of March 7, 1927. Twenty-six members of the council had appeared. Chiang Kaishek with his nearest followers stayed away.

The convention of the central executive council at Hankau was opened still under the dominancy of militarist leanings. This so-called "right" wing of the Kuo-Mintang thought it could take the session by storm if it attacked the communistic members sharply.

289

But they had underrated the growth of the power of the communists in the new territory. The communists held out. They were backed by the masses in the street which supported them by taking sides in public meetings. There were encounters between the masses and Chiang Kaishek's soldiers. Posters appeared in the streets, with the legend, "Down with Chiang Kaishek!" The leaf was turned. Chiang Kaishek's isolated regiments withdrew finally from Hankau to the opposite bank of the river. A number of generals returned to Nan-Chang; and the members of the right wing stayed away from the sessions of the council. The communistic group had the right of way. It directed the heaviest guns now against Chiang Kaishek. The convention resolved to abolish the posts of chairmen of the "standing council," and of the "military" and the "political" councils—all of which Chiang Kaishek held—and to replace them by committees of presidents. A number of councillors belonging to the right wing who were waiting, at Shanghai, for Chiang Kaishek's arrival were excluded. Even executive offices of the government now fell into the hands of the communistic group. Three new ministries were established. Three outspokenly radical communists were appointed ministers of Labour, Agriculture, and Education.

The opposition standing against the communists in the central executive council consisted, after the withdrawal of the right wing from the sessions, exclusively of the family group of Sun Yatsen. To this group belonged, apart from Sun Yatsen's wife, his brother-in-law T. V. Soong, and Eugene Chen. On the motion of Mrs. Sun Yatsen a further ministry, that of Public Health, was resolved upon; and a fifth newly-established ministry, that of Industry, was filled, on the motion of the Sun-Yatsen group, by H. H. Kung, another brother-in-law of Sun Yatsen. He was a conservative, coming from an old family of bankers in Shan-Si.

Very striking was the silence of General Tang Shengchih during all this. It was unknown to no one that he was biding his time. He was glad of Chiang Kaishek's defeat. He had the gift of waiting and all the perfidy needed for the part of a military ruler which he meant to assume over the Hankau government when the time should come.

Meanwhile Chiang Kaishek had entered Nanking.

The government of Hankau resolved to follow him

there. The capital was removed from Hankau to Nanking to put Chiang Kaishek at bay. According to all democratic customs and rules he was at this expected to resign.

But Chiang Kaishek had, on the lower Yang-Tze-Kiang, entered a dangerous atmosphere. The haze of self-righteousness which pervaded feeling at Shanghai where money interests prevailed, confirmed him in his attitude of revolt against communistic activities; the crusade which the foreigners waged swept him off his feet. His political acumen was drugged. The foreigners were no longer content to prohibit workmen's propaganda within the settlements. They right away attacked the suspicious source of all these evils, the Russian consulate, the Russian bank, and the All-Russian bureau of trade were seized and searched. At Peking, the foreign ambassadors opened the quarter of the embassies to the police of Chang Tzolin for a raid against the Russian embassy. These were actions which nearly led to open war with Russia. Yet Chiang Kaishek was led to throw aside all hesitation on his part. He went beyond all the peaceful means by which he might have gained power over the labour unions and, under his own leadership, might have induced the workmen to adopt a civil attitude with their demands. Chinese workmen are always willing to be led by friendly authority. Chiang Kaishek's generals let the soldiery loose. A frightful slaughter began among the warmed gangs of strikers at Chapei and Nantao. The offices of the unions were taken by machine-gun fire and with the bayonet; a court martial sent hundreds of arrested workmen and peasants to the place of execution, untried and uncounted.

Chiang Kaishek no longer thought of withdrawing from power. He was surrounded by generals of his army who were oligarchically inclined; at Shanghai he met with the applause of a considerable number of the most conservative members of the Kuo-Mintang; allied with these, he proclaimed at Nanking, on April 18, 1927, an anti-communistic nationalist counter government.

That was the signal for a rising of the militarist element throughout the nationalist domain.

Li Chaisam of Canton and the generals of the southern provinces declared themselves in favour of Chiang Kaishek. They drove the popular representatives of the Kuo-Mintang from civil office; they arrested the leaders of workmen and peasants and drowned every movement of these classes towards the conquest of rights within the state in blood.

An invisible line now ran, like a border line, through the nationalist army, somewhere in Kiang-Si, dividing it into two hostile camps. At Kiu-Kiang and Nan-Chang, Hankau's troops gathered under radical leaders; and at Nanking there was talk of an expedition against the middle Yang-Tze-Kiang. But the enemies faced each other for many months without letting it come to an eventful clash, for both parties, Nanking and Hankau, aimed at Peking. The thought occupied them both, by taking the northern capital, to force the foreign powers into a recognition and the nationalist rivals into a junction. Chiang Kaishek's fighting forces reached at times beyond Hsu-Cheu, on the railway from Pu-Keu to Peking. But they could not force a decision against Sun Chuan-Fang's regiments which, reorganised in northern Kiang-Su, had reappeared, and against the Shan-Tung troops of Chang Chung Chang. Chiang Kaishek lacked that knowledge of a superior military and propagandist attack on strategic points of the front, by means of which the Russians had made him a present of lightning successes in battle. At last the Nanking army had even to fall back to the right bank of the Yang-Tze-Kiang, content with defending this side of the river. The nationalist war of liberation had, under Chiang Kaishek, been reduced to the fight of the military against the militarists; and with that the nationalist cause grew limp.

Hankau on its part counted on being able to advance resistlessly on Peking as soon as an understanding of the armies of Tang Shengchih and Feng Yuhsiang could be effected. Then co-operation with the forces of Yen Shishan in the province of Shan-Si and a march against Peking would be within reach of a calculable success.

The militarists again ruined these calculations, and the triumph of the nationalist movement, already within reach, finally escaped the people.

A conference between the nationalist representatives of Hankau and Feng Yuhsiang, brought to light only militarists. Feng Yuhsiang, the very man whom the help of communistic Russia had just brought back on the stage, now also dictated the exclusion of all co-operation of communistic elements from the nationalist government. He declared himself to be of the side of Chiang Kaishek.

In a Napoleonic mandate of June 25, 1927, dated from Hsu-Cheu, Chiang Kaishek and Feng Yuhsiang revealed themselves to the people as the national heroes who had so far brought about its liberation from militarism which they by themselves also would complete.

With Feng Yuhsiang as a cover the nationalist commander-in-chief of Hankau, Tang Shengchih now dropped his mask. He led troops of Feng Yuhsiang from Chong-Cheu to Hankau; and, united with Hu-Nan detachments of his under-general Ho-Chien at Hankau, he seized the city and the government. Wholesale arrests of workmen followed. Public meetings were suppressed; the unions were dissolved. The communistic ministers and members of soviets resigned and fled.

The work of the militarists was done.

They had confiscated the reserves of the nationalist central bank at Canton and Hankau and, thereby, made the nationalist issues of paper money worthless. The financial structure of the nationalist government had crumbled. They had torn the limbs from the political body of the revolution which had just been put together out of scattered muscle and sinew, and the Kuo-Mintang had fallen changed back into loose conglomerations, scattered in rags over the country.

Borodin and the Russian advisers left the ruined field of their efforts and returned to Russia.

Shaken by the tragedy of the inability of the militarist friends to learn, but not discouraged or despairing of an ultimate victory of the cause of the common people, Mrs. Sun Yatsen, and with her the Sun Yatsen group of ministers, abandoned co-operation in the new military oligarchy which had

"turned the maxims of Sun Yatsen into their opposite; whereby the revolutionary régime had ceased to be revolutionary and become the organ which, under the banner of the revolution, restored the very order of society which the great innovator Sun Yatsen had gone out to subvert."

Again a newly arising empire lies in ruins, the world of Sun Yatsen. The foundation for the reconstruction of the Chinese empire according to the social-democratic doctrine of Sun Yatsen consisted in the active co-operation of all forces, of all classes of the people for the determination of new conditions of life; its aim, a new and real economic-political structure. As working forces for the establishment of the new structure Sun Yatsen had, on the one hand, besides a small number of capable returned students, officials and officers of the old régime; on the other, politically far from independent masses of middle-class people and proletarians from old China to build with. Among the intellectuals of both these elements there were communists, many of them from the school of Kang Yuwei. Among external things, Sun Yatsen was opposed by two different elements of resistance against his idea of the state. Firstly, by a resistance from the outside which drove him into the fight against the foreign powers; and a resistance from the inside, proceeding from the rulers of the old system which pointed towards a military fight within his own country. Secondly, by the lack of practical experience in modern state economics among his followers. This latter circumstance forced him to look for western help in the establishment of his structure. The capitalistic powers denied him that help. He found it in soviet Russia and by that was enabled to gather together, for the first time, all classes and strata of the people in the first Kuo-Mintang convention of January 1924. Among them were militarists and communists. These opposites were to permit the government party to steer its course between the dictatorship of the militarists and the dictatorship of the proletariat. A period of construction was the result. The ministers of finance and of commerce could bring about administrative and economic progress in Canton; and in a political-military sense, Sun Yatsen's cause advanced as far as the Yang-Tze-Kiang. Much of that progress was due to the methodical ways of the Russians. The Russian agents, Borodin and his associates, had renounced a bolshevist reorganisation of China. As a matter of fact, this would have been impossible. The dictatorship of the proletariat was foreign to the doctrine of Sun Yatsen; an overwhelming majority of the Kuo-Mintang would have protested against it. How far a wild communist propaganda was conducted by the Third International within the broad masses of the people, cannot be ascertained. Within the nationalist government, the Third International had no place. Nevertheless, the Russian political desires found their count; for in the fight of Sun Yatsen arose a China which turned away from capitalistic ways: a bulwark for Russia. The claims of the militarists to power within the nationalist government were the cause of the growth of the communistic group, of the violent fight between the two movements, and of the exclusion of the communistic group which involved the exclusion of the creative forces of the centre. The foundation has been cracked.

But militarism in the ranks of the Kuo-Mintang is sterile, as all Chinese militarism: it is a destructive power only. Escaped from the "word" which had been hanging above them like a sword of Damocles or like a star, the generals began at once to make war among themselves. Tang Shengchih declared himself to be against Chiang Kaishek. Feng Yuhsiang confirmed the latter in his attitude towards the former; out of the fight of the two against each other, he hoped to win the Yang-Tze cities as easy loot for himself. Chiang Kaishek soon found himself in a difficult position. He resigned the command-in-chief over the government of Nanking.

Militarism within the Kuo-Mintang will still be vanquished, whichever way it be; for the ideas of a liberation from autocracy, of a share in the determination of the conditions of its own life, of a deliverance from the power of the propertied classes over the living life of the common people, are working deeply in the masses.

All times have fought for freedom; every age for a freedom of its own; and the Chinese people will fight on for its special freedom.

Without freedom, what were the world?

INDEX

301

INDEX

Shikai, Yuan, 64, 67-8; urges regent to abdicate, 69; becomes president of Kuo-Mintang, 69; becomes president, 70, 75, 76; his death, 77

Shishan, Yen, 137-8, 245

Siutsuen, Hung, 34

Soong, T. V., 177-9, 180, 226-7, 253-4

Sun Yatsen, death of, 57; effect of ideas of, 59, 60; youth of, 60; college days of, 60-1; attempts revolution, 65; returns from exile, 66; elected president, 66; dream of freedom, 69; abdicates presidency, 70; his idealism a pious illusion, 74; in exile again, 76; returns to Canton, 79; tries to better economic conditions, 80-2; forced to flee revolutionaries, 88-9; rule of his life, 90; peculiarity of character of, 95-7; no communistic aims, 99; doctrine of, 100-5; bequest of, 105-8; wife of, 109-11; philosophy of life of, 124-5; personality of, 130; influence of Russia on, 132-3; rumor of unnatural death, 144; funeral of, 145-6; his belief in sacred relations, 158-9; later bias toward Soviet, 163-5; as guiding genius of Nationalist government, 168-9; on value of family organization, 222-4; summary of, 297-300

Taft, President, 73

Tingfang, Wu, 68, 79, 81

Trotzki, 217

Tung, Huan, 66, 77

Tzolin, Chang, 133-5, 140-1, 148-9, 152, 189, 191, 197-9, 200-4, 246-7, 249, 250

Washington Conference, 188-9, 228

World War, 54, 130, 160, 187, 255

Wu, Dr. C. C., 126-7

Wu, Prince, 122-3

Yen, W. W., 205

Yuan-Hung, Li, Colonel, 66, 68

Yuhsiang, Feng, 136, 147-8, 152, 196-7, 200-5, 244, 246, 248, 295, 300

Yungsiang, Lu, 138-9, 140, 142

Yuren, Chen (*see* Eugene Chen)

Yuwei, K'ang, 63

302

SOVIET RUSSIA

MANCHURIA

MONGOLIA

KIRIN

GREAT WALL

ORDOS

CHILI

KOREA

TIBET

KAN-SU

SHAN-SI

SHAN-TUNG

SHEN-SI

HO-NAN

NGAN-HWEI

SHANGHAI

HU-PE

SZE-CHUAN

YANG-TZE-KIANG

CHE-KIANG

KIANG-SI

KWEI-CHEU

FU-KIANG

YUN NAN

KWANG-SI

CANTON

KWANG-TUNG

FORMOSA "JAPAN"

HONGKONG

Sketch Map of CHINA

JOHN M. MEEKISON